BATTLETECH®

TECHNICAL READOUT: 2750

FASA CORPORATION

·

1989

TECHNICAL READOUT: 2750

Writing
Clare W. Hess
Dale L. Kemper
Jim Long
Blaine L. Pardoe
Boy F. Petersen Jr.

Development
Sam Lewis

Editorial Staff
Editor-in-Chief
L. Ross Babcock III
Senior Editor
Donna Ippolito
Editor
Jim Musser
Editorial Assistant
C. R. Green
Research Assistant
Kent Stolt

Production Staff
Production Manager
Sam Lewis
Art Director
Dana Knutson
Cover Art
Dana Knutson
Technical Assistance
Bob McElmeel
Technical Designs
Dana Knutson
Tom Miller
Michael Weaver
Illustrations
Dana Knutson
Personal Equipment
Steve Venters

Published by FASA Corporation
P. O. Box 6930
Chicago, IL 60680
Corrected Second Printing

TABLE OF CONTENTS

STAR LEAGUE TECHNOLOGY

In the closing years of the Star League, great strides were made in all areas of military technology. Improvements in weaponry, armor, and 'Mech manufacturing techniques created a deadly fighting machine that was faster, better-armed, and better-protected than any of its predecessors. Though some weapons systems using these technological breakthroughs were seen on the battlefield in the latter days of the League, the underlying technology had sometimes not fully matured. As a consequence, these systems were costly, bulky, and in some cases, mutually exclusive.

The collapse of the Star League and the start of the Succession Wars cut short further refinements of these technologies. The Inner Sphere's industrial base was shattered by invading armies, while many skilled technicians died on the front trying to keep the remaining machines in operation. The complex machinery that turned out these jewels of technology was ground into the dust under the massive juggernauts it had helped to create. The Successor Lords had no choice but to use older, obsolescent technologies in their war machines. Over the years, the constant warfare that plagued the worlds of the Inner Sphere kept the Successor States from gaining the respite needed to rebuild their industrial base to pre-war levels. As time passed, there was less and less to rebuild and fewer and fewer who knew how to do it.

All that has changed. Thanks to the Gray Death Legion's discovery of a Star League computer library core on Helm in 3028, much lost knowledge has been regained. After 20 years of research and experimentation, aided by the Gray Death memory core, the Federated Commonwealth, the Draconis Combine, and the Free Worlds League are all on the verge of fielding 'Mechs using technology not seen for centuries.

This Technical Readout is compiled from data contained in the Gray Death memory core, providing information on the most advanced military equipment ever known to man. Wherever possible, a full range of technical and historical data is provided. In some cases, the complete loss of historical records did not permit a detailed discussion of the equipment. There are also occasional Editor's Notes to clarify, expand, or explain certain details when necessary.

STAR LEAGUE TECHNOLOGY

WEAPONS

Unless otherwise noted, these weapons can be used by vehicles of all types.

ANTI-MISSILE SYSTEM

The Anti-Missile System is a short-ranged, rapid-fire, point-defense machine gun capable of tracking, engaging, and destroying incoming missiles. Though very effective, the system's main drawback is its high ammunition consumption. Many pilots of Anti-Missile-equipped 'Mechs have attempted to engage incoming flights of missiles, only to find that their ammo bins have long since run dry.

Game Use

Whenever a 'Mech equipped with an Anti-Missile System is attacked by a flight of missiles, the player can choose to engage the system prior to the To-Hit Roll. The defending player simply rolls 1D6 to determine how many missiles the system has destroyed. The player rolls another 1D6 and multiplies the result by 2 to determine how much anti-missile ammunition was spent shooting down the attacking missiles. Note that it is possible for the second die roll to result in more ammunition being expended than was available. In such a case, the results of the missiles destroyed roll still apply.

The missiles then make their attack as normal, *if* any remain, but the player uses the column appropriate to their reduced number on the Missile Hit Table. If the number of missiles falls between two columns, use the column closest to the number, rounding down. For example, an LRM 10 flight that was reduced to 9 missiles would still use the 10 column, but if that flight was reduced to 8 missiles, it would use the 6 column. A flight reduced to 1 missile uses the 2 column. A flight cannot hit with more missiles than it has after the attack, regardless of the result on the Missile Hit Table.

The Anti-Missile System can only be used against missiles.

ANTI-MISSILE SYSTEM		
Tonnage	Critical Spaces	Shots/Ton
.5	1	12

ARROW IV MISSILE SYSTEM

The Arrow IV missile is a long-range surface-to-surface missile designed to supplement standard conventional artillery such as the Long Tom and Sniper. The main advantage of the Arrow IV system is its relatively lightweight design, compared to conventional artillery. The major drawback is the high cost of its ammunition.

The Arrow IV system uses two types of missiles. The most common and least expensive is the standard area-saturation missile. This is used to attack area targets, doing general explosive damage to any object within a 45-meter blast radius.

The other type of missile actively homes in on a single target, doing only a small amount of collateral damage. This missile carries special targeting equipment that allows it to home in on TAG-designated targets.

Game Use

Arrow IV missile artillery is treated just like any other artillery piece, using all the Offboard Artillery Rules found on pages 41–2 of the **BattleTech Manual**, unless otherwise noted below.

If a standard area-saturation missile is fired, the location of the target hex and the turn of arrival should be noted on paper. The area saturation missiles do 20 points of damage to all units in the impact hex and 10 points to all units in the surrounding hexes.

Homing missiles do not need to have a target hex plotted when fired, but the attacker must note which TAG (Target Acquisition Gear)-equipped unit he will use for designating during the turn of arrival. During the Offboard Artillery portion of the phase on the turn of arrival, the attacking player must designate a target with the unit previously noted. If the unit does not designate a target, the missile will impact harmlessly into the ground.

To designate a target, a TAG-equipped unit must have a valid LOS to the target and be within 15 hexes. The Base To-Hit Number is found on the table below. All normal combat modifiers for attacks apply, including attacker's movement, target movement, partial cover, *Gunnery* Skill, and so on.

If the target is designated, the missile strikes the target on a 2D6 roll of 4 or more. It will do 20 points of damage to the target and 5 points of normal artillery damage to any other unit in the hex. The damage location is discovered *as though the designating unit were firing at the target*. Therefore, if the designating unit is in the left-side arc of the target, use the left-side column of the Hit Location Table to find out what portion of the 'Mech was hit.

If the attack misses, it does only 5 points of artillery damage to the target and to any other unit in the hex.

ARROW IV MISSILE SYSTEM						
Heat	Damage	Minimum	Max Range	Tonnage	Critical	Ammo
10	20/10*	Artillery	5	15	15	5
* See Homing Arrow IV						

			TAG					
Heat	Damage	Minimum	Short	Medium	Long	Tonnage	Critical	Ammo
0	NA	–	1–5	6–9	10–15	1	1	NA

EXTENDED RANGE LARGE LASER AND PPC

These weapons improve on the basic large laser and PPC with the addition of superior beam focusing and targeting equipment. Though this significantly increases range for the weapons, they do the same damage as their less sophisticated cousins and generate approximately 50 percent more heat when fired.

EXTENDED RANGE WEAPONS

	Heat	Damage	Minimum	Short	Medium	Long	Tonnage	Critical	Ammo
ER Large Laser	12	8	—	1 – 7	8 – 14	15 – 19	5	2	—
ER PPC	15	10	—	1 – 7	8 – 14	15 – 23	7	3	—

GAUSS RIFLE

The Gauss Rifle uses a series of magnets to propel the shell through the barrel toward the target. Though the weapon requires a great deal of power to operate, it generates very little heat and can accelerate a projectile to muzzle velocities twice that of conventional weapon systems.

GAUSS RIFLE

Heat	Damage	Minimum	Short	Medium	Long	Tonnage	Critical	Ammo
1	15	2	1 – 7	8 – 15	16 – 22	15	7	10

KWI ULTRA AUTOCANNON 5

The Kawabata Weapons Inc. Autocannon 5 Ultra resembles the standard AC/5 only in the general amount of damage that each round can inflict. The Ultra boasts a shorter, smooth-bore barrel, a modified breech mechanism, a rapid-feed ammo reloader, and specially designed ammunition. These enhancements create an AC/5 of normal tonnage and heat output that has a reduced minimum range, extended maximum range, and can shoot at either normal and double rates of fire.

Game Use

Whenever the player fires the AC/5 Ultra, he can choose to fire at normal or double rate of fire. If he selects normal rate of fire, all normal combat rules apply. If he chooses double rate of fire, use the rules given below.

An AC/5 Ultra firing at double rate generates twice as many heat points and uses two shots of ammunition instead of one. The standard To-Hit Roll is made. If the roll is successful, the player must roll in the "2" column of the Missile Hit Table to determine how many shots hit. For each hit on the target, roll to discover the hit location. Each shot that hits does 5 points of damage.

Additionally, whenever the weapon fires in its double-fire mode and the result of the To-Hit Roll is a 2, the arming circuitry fails and the weapon is useless until repaired by a Tech. To make this repair, roll 2D6. On a result of 3 or more, the weapon is completely repaired in a required time of 15 minutes, per the Repair Rules and Table on page 92 of **MechWarrior**.

AUTOCANNON 5 ULTRA

Heat	Damage	Minimum	Short	Medium	Long	Tonnage	Critical	Ammo
1	5	2	1 – 6	7 – 13	14 – 20	9	5	20

LB 10-X AUTOCANNON

This weapon is closely related to the common AC/10. The design of the LB 10-X uses several types of lightweight, rapid-heat-dissipation alloys. Though this makes the weapon costlier, its lighter weight and need for fewer heat sinks easily makes up for the expense. Another important feature of the LB 10-X is its Mercury-IV fire control equipment. This electronic system gives the cannon a better hit probability at all ranges, as well as extending its maximum effective range by 20 percent.

In addition to firing standard Dual-Purpose Armor-Defeating Rounds, the weapon may also fire a special Cluster Round that acts much like an anti-'Mech shotgun. After being fired, the round breaks up into several smaller submunitions. This improves the chance of striking a critical location on the target, but also reduces the overall damage done and spreads it out over the entire target area rather than concentrating it in one location.

Game Use

The player must specify at the start of the game which LB 10-X ammo is cluster-type ammunition and which is normal ammunition. LB 10-X Cluster Rounds can only be designated in full-ton lots. When firing the ammunition, the player marks off the appropriate type.

Any attacks made with the Cluster Round receive a −1 modifier to the To-Hit Number at all ranges. Resolve hits by Cluster Rounds like a missile hit, with the player rolling on the 10 column of the Missile Hit Table to determine how many of the submunitions actually strike the target. Make a separate Hit Location Roll for each of the sub-munitions that strike. Each successful hit does 1 point of damage to the location struck.

				LB 10-X				
Heat	Damage	Minimum	Short	Medium	Long	Tonnage	Critical	Ammo
2	10	−	1 − 6	7 − 12	13 − 18	11	6	10

ONE-SHOT MISSILE PACKS

It is possible for a vehicle or 'Mech to be equipped with a single-shot version of the standard missile launcher. Such a missile system is designated by an "OS" after the missile nomenclature.

Game Use

Single shot launchers weigh half a ton more than standard missile-launchers, but the launcher incorporates a single shot or volley of missiles into that weight. The player does not need to purchase any other ammunition for the launcher. The launcher can be fired only once in a game.

PULSE LASER

The Pulse Laser uses a rapid-cycling, high-energy pulse to generate multiple laser beams, creating a machine-gun effect that improves the weapon's hit probabilities. The weapon weighs more and generates slightly higher heat than its beam-firing counterparts, and increases their average damage. The Pulse Laser also tends to be shorter-ranged. Many soldiers think that the increased hit probabilities are worth any drawbacks to the weapon.

Game Use

Pulse lasers are used in the same manner as normal weapons, but an automatic −2 applies to the Base To-Hit Number.

When playing **BattleTroops**, the Small Pulse Laser can function as an automatic weapon.

	Heat	Damage	Minimum	Short	Medium	Long	Tonnage	Critical	Ammo
				PULSE LASERS					
Small Pulse Laser	2	3	−	1	2	3	1	1	—
Medium Pulse Laser	4	6	−	1 − 2	3 − 4	5 − 6	2	1	—
Large Pulse Laser	10	9	−	1 − 3	4 − 7	8 − 10	7	2	—

STREAK SRM-2

This short-range missile launcher is linked to a Targa/7 fire-control system. The SRMs will automatically hit any target locked onto by the Targa system.

Game Use

Before the Streak can fire, it must have a lock-on. To obtain a lock-on, the player makes a standard To-Hit Roll, just as when firing a normal SRM, during his turn of the Combat Phase. If successful, the player may immediately fire his SRMs at the locked-on target. Both SRMs will automatically hit, and the player rolls in the usual way to determine hit locations. If the lock-on roll fails, the player does not need to fire the SRMs or build up any heat. The player must roll for a lock-on each turn, even if he achieved a lock-on the previous turn.

SWARM LRMS

Swarm LRMs are special long-range missiles that use hundreds of submunitions to saturate an area with devastating firepower.

Game Use

At the start of play, players should note whether or not their LRM ammunition is Swarm-type. LRM ammunition can be designated as Swarm only in full-ton lots.

Swarm LRMs operate like normal LRMs except that those missing their target will attack any units, friendly or enemy, that are adjacent or in the same hex as the original target. Any missile that misses may attack the closest unit adjacent to the original target, and then the next closest unit adjacent to the original target, and so on. A new modified To-Hit Number is recalculated based on the new target's range, movement, and other determining factors. If there are two or more targets at the same distance from the original target, the defending player may choose the order of attacks. Use the closest column on the Missile Hit Table, rounding down, to resolve each attack.

For example, an LRM-20 equipped with Swarms fires at a target adjacent to two other units. The LRM 20 misses, and the defending player chooses an adjacent unit for the next attack. This attack has a new modified To-Hit Number, and 15 LRMs hit the target. The remaining 5 LRMs are then used against the other adjacent target. They miss and so are lost.

Swarm LRMs are fired and used as normal LRMs except that they cost three times as much.

THUNDER LRMS

Thunder LRMs are used to deliver scatterable mine fields. Each round contains five small anti-vehicle and anti-personnel mines.

Game Use

Players should note at the start of the game whether their LRM ammunition is Thunder-type or not. LRM ammunition can be designated as Thunder-type only in full-ton lots.

Thunder LRM attacks use all the normal LRM rules except that, like artillery, the attack is always launched against a hex rather than against a unit. Thus, a Thunder LRM attack is only modified by the attacker's movement and terrain, never by the movement of a unit that happens to be in the target hex.

If the attack misses, it scatters, per normal Artillery Rules. Thunder LRM attacks that hit leave the target hex mined with a minefield equal in strength to the number of missiles in the attack. Thus, an LRM 20 will lay a 20-point minefield, and an LRM 5 will lay a 5-point minefield. Units, friendly or enemy, in a hex hit by a Thunder attack are not affected until they move out of the hex. At that point, the player must make a die roll to see if he steps on a mine. All other units that enter the hex during their movement must also roll to see if they step on a mine. Use the rules found on page 45, Conventional Mine Fields, of the **BattleTech Manual** to resolve the attack, remembering that the attack's value varies with the size of the LRM launcher.

STREAK SRM-2								
Heat	Damage	Minimum	Short	Medium	Long	Tonnage	Critical	Ammo
2	*	—	1 – 3	4 – 6	7 – 9	1.5	1	50

ELECTRONICS

Except for the Myomer Accelerator Signal Circuitry, which is usable only by 'Mechs, this equipment can be used by vehicles of all types.

ARTEMIS IV FCS

The Artemis IV is a fire-control system that improves the accuracy of any short- or long-range missile systems that a 'Mech or vehicle might carry. Mounted in a dome on the side of the missile launcher, the Artemis IV locks onto any target designated by the pilot, illuminates the location with an IR beam, and fires a spread of missiles. The system provides mid-course correction data to the missiles via tight-beam, microwave communications link. The Artemis IV is not completely foolproof and cannot compensate for inadequate *Gunnery* Skill. The Artemis guides the missiles to whatever the pilot's crosshairs are targeting when he fires the missile, be it 'Mech, vehicle, rock, or tree.

Game Use

The Artemis IV can be mounted with any long- or short-range missile pack, with one Artemis system per missile pack required. All the 'Mech's missile systems must have the Artemis or none can have it.

The Artemis IV is incompatible with the Streak SRM-2 system, the Narc Missile Beacon, and the Swarm and Thunder LRM missiles. Additionally, the Artemis IV requires a special version of the standard SRM and LRM missiles. For game purposes, these special missiles differ from normal missiles only in cost, which is doubled.

Any missile launch from an Artemis-equipped 'Mech is treated exactly like a normal attack, except that if the attack hits, apply a +2 modifier when consulting the Missile Hit Table. This has the effect of increasing the number of hits on the target.

An Artemis IV system weighs one ton and takes up one critical space.

BEAGLE ACTIVE PROBE

The Beagle Active Probe is the most advanced sensor system in the Inner Sphere. Capable of detecting and identifying even shut-down and camouflaged units at distances much greater than normal electronic warfare suites, the Beagle is a valued addition to any recon unit.

Game Use

A 'Mech equipped with a Beagle Active Probe automatically gives a **BattleForce** lance an Active Electronic Probe chit. On the **BattleTech** map, a 'Mech so equipped will detect any hidden 'Mech or vehicle (not infantry) if it moves within four hexes of the unit's location, and would have a valid LOS to the hex in which the unit is hiding.

BEAGLE ACTIVE PROBE	
Tonnage	Critical Spaces
1.5	2

GUARDIAN ECM SUITE

The Guardian ECM Suite is a broad-spectrum jamming and electronic countermeasure device, designed to reduce the efficiency of enemy long-range scanning and surveillance equipment. The Guardian interferes with sensor readings, preventing identification at ranges of more than 180 meters. Closer than that, 'Mech pilots usually rely on their own vision in case their sensors cannot override the Guardian's jamming.

Game Use

A lance with a 'Mech equipped with a Guardian ECM Suite automatically receives an ECM chit in **BattleForce**.

GUARDIAN ECM SUITE	
Tonnage	Critical Spaces
1.5	2

MYOMER ACCELERATOR SIGNAL CIRCUITRY (MASC)

The MASC system is a device that increases a 'Mech's short-term speed. It works by boosting the electronic signal to the myomer muscles, which makes them contract more rapidly than normal. The system is effective in increasing the 'Mech's overall speed, but it can stress a 'Mech's legs to the point of catastrophic failure of the various actuators, especially if used for too long a period.

Game Use

Any player with a MASC-equipped 'Mech can announce that he is activating the system at the start of his Movement Phase. The player rolls 2D6. On a result of 3 or more, the system works and the 'Mech is running at a speed twice its normal walking speed. On a result of 2, the leg actuators freeze up and the 'Mech is immobile for the rest of the game.

If the player chooses to use the system the next turn, the activating roll is increased by 2, to 5 or greater. The third turn of consecutive use increases the activating roll by 4, the fourth turn by 8, and the fifth turn results in automatic failure of the legs.

Players can reduce the activating number by not utilizing the system. For each turn that the system is not used, the number is reduced to the next lower step. For example, if a player used the MASC for three consecutive turns (giving it an activating target number of 7), one turn of non-use would reduce the activating number to 5, and two turns of non-use would reduce the target number back to the original 3. The activating number can never fall below 3.

MASC SYSTEM	
Tonnage	Critical Spaces
Mech Tonnage/20*	Mech Tonnage/20*
*Round to nearest whole number	

NARC MISSILE BEACON

The Narc Missile Beacon uses special missiles, called pods, which are powerful homing beacons mounted behind a magnetic head. When a hit is achieved, the pod emits a homing signal for other Narc-equipped missiles. Like the Artemis system, the Narc vastly increases the number of hits from any missile barrage. Unlike the Artemis IV, the lock is never broken, because the transmitter is attached to the target 'Mech.

Game Use

Players may fire one Narc Pod per launcher each turn as a normal SRM attack. If the attack is successful, the pod attaches to the target 'Mech. In any following Combat Phase, any successful missile attacks by a Narc-equipped unit add a +2 to the roll against the Missile Hit Table. This effect stays with the targeted 'Mech for the length of the game.

The Narc system is incompatible with the Artemis IV system, the Streak SRM-2 system, and the Swarm and Thunder LRM missiles. Additionally, the cost of missiles for a Narc-equipped unit is doubled, because its operation requires a modified version of the standard free-flight SRM and LRM missiles.

NARC MISSILE BEACON								
Heat	Damage	Minimum	Short	Medium	Long	Tonnage	Critical	Ammo
0	NA	–	1 – 3	4 – 6	7 – 9	3	2	6

CONSTRUCTION MATERIALS

Unless otherwise noted, the following materials may only be used in the construction of BattleMechs.

CELLULAR AMMUNITION STORAGE EQUIPMENT (CASE)

CASE is a damage-control technology designed to mitigate the effects of an ammunition explosion. The system consists of layered Ferro-Fibrous plates along five of the six sides of the storage compartment. In the event of an explosion, the stronger Ferro-Fibrous plates contain the blast, channeling the force toward the back of the 'Mech. The loading doors blow open, releasing the force of the blast away from the 'Mech. In practice, this will destroy the armor plating on the back section of the 'Mech and damage or destroy any components housed near the CASE system. Though it destroys the torso section, the system protects the vital engine area, allowing the pilot to continue fighting or to exit the battlefield.

Game Use

The CASE system can be built into either torso side of a 'Mech. It does take up one critical space in the section where it is mounted and weighs half a ton. Treat hits to the critical space where the CASE system is located as "no result" and make a new die roll.

Any onboard ammunition that explodes in that section will do normal damage to the internal structure of that section. Excess damage is then applied to the *back* armor of the section. Any other remaining damage is not applied. Remember that if all the internal structure on either side of the torso is destroyed, the corresponding arm will not work.

CASE systems can only be mounted on 'Mechs or vehicles. In vehicles, the system can only be mounted in the body location. Any ammunition explosion results in the destruction of the back armor and puts the vehicle out of action. However, any crewmember or passengers in the vehicle will survive the explosion.

CASE SYSTEM	
Tonnage	Critical Spaces
.5	1

DOUBLE HEAT SINKS

Double Heat Sinks are the ultimate in heat-dissipation technology, with a heat-to-weight efficiency ratio twice that of previous generations. They are three times as bulky as the standard heat sink, however. Though not a problem if mounted in a 'Mech's torso, there is not enough room for them in a Mech's legs. Because the two heat-dissipation technologies are not compatible, designers must make a trade-off between greater heat dissipation and more room for weapon systems.

A bracketed number next to the heat sink number in the 'Mech's statistics indicates double heat sinks.

Game Use

'Mechs with double heat sinks dissipate 2 points of heat for each operating heat sink each turn. If submerged in water, the heat sink will dissipate 4 points of heat each turn. A 'Mech cannot be equipped with both single and double heat sinks. Vehicles cannot be equipped with double heat sinks.

DOUBLE HEAT SINKS	
Tonnage	Critical Spaces
1	3

ENDO STEEL INTERNAL STRUCTURE

Endo Steel was specially designed for use in 'Mech skeletons. Constructed by Zero-G manufacturing techniques that uniformly mix high-density steel with lower-density titanium and aluminum, the resulting metal is twice as strong per unit of weight as standard skeleton materials but considerably bulkier.

Game Use

'Mechs that use Endo Steel need allocate only half the normal weight to their Internal Structure (keeping all fractions). However, the bulk of this alloy reduces the number of free critical spaces by 14. The player can allocate this amount as he sees fit, even filling up one section totally, as long as a total of 14 Critical Hit locations are filled in by the Endo Steel. A hit to a critical space taken up by the Endo Steel structure is treated as "no result" and should be rerolled.

FERRO-FIBROUS ARMOR

Ferro-Fibrous Armor is an improved version of normal 'Mech armor. Utilizing a weave of ferro-steel and ferro-titanium fibers, this armor plating increases tensile strength by 12 percent, compared to older types of armor plating. Ferro-Fibrous armor is much bulkier than an equivalent weight of normal armor plating, however. A version known as Ferro-Aluminum armor is also available for AeroSpace Fighters.

Game Use

'Mechs that use Ferro-Fibrous Armor increase their Armor Factor. Calculate the Armor Factor as normal, then multiply by 1.12, dropping all fractions. This is the 'Mech's total Armor Factor. The bulk of the armor reduces the number of free critical spaces by 14. The player can allocate this amount as he sees fit, even filling up one section totally if desired. A total of 14 Critical Hit locations must be filled in by the Ferro-Fibrous Armor. Hits to a critical space taken up by Ferro-Fibrous Armor are treated as "no result" and should be rerolled.

Ferro-Fibrous Armor may also be used in vehicles and AeroSpace Fighters. In such cases, it reduces by 2 the maximum number of weapons and ammo that can be mounted in each side.

XL ENGINE TECHNOLOGY

Advances in fusion power plant shielding have allowed designers to retrofit their standard engines with new and lighter shielding materials. The net result is a vastly decreased overall engine weight, though once again, at the expense of compactness.

Game Use

Players may designate any fusion plant as being equipped with XL technology. The result is that the normal engine weight is half (retain fractions) the published amount. The player must allocate three critical spaces for the Engine to *both* the left and the right torso of the Critical Hit Table of the 'Mech. Any hit to these new locations is treated as a normal Engine Hit. XL Technology is not available for AeroSpace Fighters or vehicles.

EQUIPMENT TABLE

Type	Heat	Damage	Min	Short	Medium	Long	Tonnage	Critical	Ammo
Weapons									
Anti-Missile System	1	*					.5	1	12
Arrow IV System	10	20/10*			Artillery	5	15	15	5
ER Large Laser	12	8	–	1 – 7	8 – 14	15 – 19	5	2	
ER PPC	15	10	–	1 – 7	8 – 14	15 – 23	7	3	
Gauss Rifle	1	15	2	1 – 7	8 – 15	16 – 22	15	7	10
KWI Ultra AC/5	1	5	2	1 – 6	7 – 13	14 – 20	9	5	20
LB 10-X A/C	2	10	–	1 – 6	7 – 12	13 – 18	11	6	10
Narc Missile Beacon	0	NA	–	1 – 3	4 – 6	7 – 9	3	2	6
Pulse Laser (Lg.)	10	9	–	1 – 3	4 – 7	8 – 10	7	2	
Pulse Laser (Med.)	4	6	–	1 – 2	3 – 4	5 – 6	2	1	
Pulse Laser (Sm.)	2	3	–	1	2	3	1	1	
Streak SRM-2	2	*	–	1 – 3	4 – 6	7 – 9	1.5	1	50
Other Equipment									
Artemis IV FCS							1	1	
Beagle Active Probe							1.5	2	
CASE							.5	1	
Double Heat Sink							1	3	
Guardian ECM Suite							1.5	2	
MASC							Mech Tonnage/20*	Mech Tonnage/20*	
TAG	0	*	–	1 – 5	6 – 9	10 – 15	1	1	

*See special rules for this equipment.

COSTS

Players should note that these costs are for comparison purposes only. This technology has yet to reach general distribution.

EQUIPMENT COST TABLE

	Cost	Reloads
Anti-Missile System	100,000	2,000/ton
Arrow IV System	450,000	10,000/ton(standard), 15,000/ton (homing)
Artemis IV FCS	100,000	2x normal missile cost
Beagle Active Probe	200,000	
CASE	50,000	
Double Heat Sink	6,000 each (include 10 that come with engine)	
Endo Steel II	4x normal Skeleton Cost	
ER Large Laser	200,000	
ER PPC	300,000	
Ferro-Fibrous Armor	20,000 x Tons of armor	
Gauss Rifle	300,000	20,000/ton
Guardian ECM Suite	200,000	
KWI Ultra AC/5	200,000	9,000/ton
LB 10-X	400,000	12,000/ton 20,000/ton (Cluster)
MASC	1000 x Engine Rating x Tonnage	
Narc Missile Beacon 100,000	6,000/ton	
Pulse Laser (Lg.)	175,000	
Pulse Laser (Med.)	60,000	
Pulse Laser (Sm.)	16,000	
Streak SRM-2	15,000	54,000/ton
Swarm LRM	2x normal missile cost	
TAG	50,000	
Thunder LRM	2x normal missile cost	
XL Engine	4x normal engine cost	

BATTLEMECHS

Mass: 20 tons
Chassis: Bergan MXII
Power Plant: LTV 160 (MASC)
Cruising Speed: 86 kph
Maximum Speed: 130 kph
Jump Jets: None
   Jump Capacity: None
Armor: Mitchell-091 Ferro-Fibrous
Armament:
   2 Martell Medium Lasers
   2 Hessen IX Small Lasers
Manufacturer: Mitchell Vehicles
Communications System: DataTech 401
Targeting and Tracking System: Skyhunter IV

Overview:

The unveiling of the *Mercury* was heralded as the dawn of a new age in BattleMech design. Billed as an obvious successor to the aging *Stinger* and *Wasp*, the *Mercury* answered many dreams of scout lance pilots. Initial specifications called for the light 'Mech to be faster and better armed than any other in its class, all without a reduction in armor.

Displayed for the first time in 2742, the *Mercury* was an electronic marvel, the showpiece of the Star League Defense Forces. At the unveiling, Mitchell Vehicles spokesmen described multiple break-through systems only in general terms, and none of the new 'Mechs was allowed outside the direct control of the Regular Army. [EDITOR'S NOTE: Just before the Exodus, the new *Mercury* 'Mechs remained with units stationed on Terra and at the factory on Graham IV. These all left with General Kerensky. The highest concentration to remain behind were with the Eighth Recon Battalion of the Third Regimental Combat Team, known as the Eridani Light Horse, which became a renowned mercenary unit. The Eighth lost all twelve of its *Mercury* 'Mechs during fighting on Sendai in 2798.]

Capabilities:

The heart of the *Mercury* is the Myomer Accelerator Signal Circuitry (MASC) system. Acting as a "turbocharger" for the myomer bundles in the legs, the MASC system allows the *Mercury* to reach speeds of up to 172 kph in short bursts. The special circuitry sends shorter but stronger signals to the myomer bundles, effectively doubling the *Mercury's* walking speed. Long-term use can damage the 'Mech's actuators, but timely use in critical situations can mean the difference between life and death.

With its high speed and energy weapons, the *Mercury* is an ideal scout and raider, capable of remaining in the field for as long as the pilot is able to take the stresses of battle.

The few critics of the design point out the *Mercury's* lack of jump jets. Despite this drawback, the *Mercury* is well accepted by the Star League commanders. Though comparable in weight to the *Stinger* or *Wasp*, the *Mercury* can survive longer in battle because of its heavier weapons and the stronger Ferro-Fibrous armor.

The energy-dissipation system is a marvel of Star League technology. Automated heat sinks monitor themselves and channel excess heat away from the reactor and cockpit.

The Hessen IX Small Lasers in the head and the center torso are a matched pair. The lasers are slipped into place, bolted down, and connected in three places to the power circuits and cooling feeds. If the lasers are damaged or destroyed, the bolts can be removed and the entire system replaced, usually in minutes. [EDITOR'S NOTE: This modular replacement system was expected to revolutionize the logistical support of field units, but the Exodus and First Succession War put an end to any radical departure from standard military procedure.]

Though both Martell Medium Lasers use the same type of barrel and targeting feeds, they do differ greatly in their power systems. The right arm laser diffuses the power all along the upper and lower arm, housing redundant systems in both sections to provide backup capabilities should one part of the arm be damaged. The torso mount, however, clusters the entire system into a compact area. Any damage to the torso, other than a direct hit on the power system, is likely to pass through, missing the laser entirely.

Type: **MCY-99 Mercury**

Equipment		Mass
Internal Structure:		2
Engine: LTV 160 (MASC)		6
Walking MP:	8	
Running MP:	12 (16)	
Jumping MP:	0	
Heat Sinks:	10	0
Gyro:		2
Cockpit:		3
Armor Factor:	54	3

	Internal Structure	Armor Value
Head	3	5
Center Torso	6	7
Center Torso (rear)		4
R/L Torso	5	6
R/L Torso (rear)		2
R/L Arm	3	5
R/L Leg	4	6

Weapons and Ammo:	Location	Critical	
Medium Laser	RA	1	1
Medium Laser	LT	1	1
Small Laser	CT	1	0.5
Small Laser	H	1	0.5
MASC	CT	1	1

Mass: 20 tons
Chassis: Chariot Type II
Power Plant: GM 120
Cruising Speed: 65 kph
Maximum Speed: 97 kph
Jump Jets: None
    Jump Capacity: None
Armor: Armorscale, with CASE
Armament:
    1 Zeus-5 LRM Launcher
    2 Hellion Spitfire Medium Lasers
Manufacturer: Ford Military Limited
Communications System: Opus I Ultrabeam
Targeting and Tracking System: Orion 80

Overview:

The *Thorn* is an older BattleMech design, incorporated into the Hegemony Armed Forces during the late 24th Century. It was the first 'Mech to incorporate the Endo Steel II Skeleton. The *Thorn* was unveiled with tremendous hype, but initial reviews were mixed. Commanders later agreed that Endo Steel II had obvious advantages but would not be suitable for all 'Mechs.

The *Thorn* was designed to serve in front-line combat units. Its inability to jump was not considered unusual for this type of duty, but commanders who tried to use all light 'Mechs as scouts found the *Thorn* to be useless. Once separated from company mates, the *Thorn*'s heavier armor and greater firepower were no match for a quicker opponent.

Capabilities:

The *Thorn* has had mixed reviews for the entire length of its service. Supporters point out that the design packs more punch per ton than any other 'Mech and that its armor is also the best of its size. In a toe-to-toe slugfest, the *Thorn* can usually reduce an equal weight opponent to scrap in minutes.

Opponents of the design note that a 'Mech cannot hit what it cannot reach. Although the 120 Class engine allows the 'Mech to run at a respectable speed, its lack of jump jets leaves the *Thorn* in the dust of other light 'Mechs. The Zeus Long-Range Missile system only partially offsets this lack of pursuit ability.

This favoring of armor and weapons over maneuverability has made the *Thorn* a favorite of front-line light companies.

The weapon placement and ease of maintenance have given the design high marks in every technician's manual. The arms and legs are completely accessible, allowing a service crew to actually enter the limbs and work on repairs from the inside.

The *Thorn*'s main armament consists of twin medium lasers. These identical weapons further improve maintenance and are extremely efficient. The design is noted as a "cool running" 'Mech, but the placement of one laser directly under the pilot's feet makes the *Thorn* seem to be running hotter than it really is. Extensive cooling is provided in the cockpit area, but the lack of an effective venting system for the medium laser makes repeated firing uncomfortable for the pilot.

The Zeus Long-Range Missile system is extremely accurate, and the arm mount allows the pilot to switch targets quickly. If damaged, the entire system can be replaced in a few hours, which is fortunate, as the launcher can easily be destroyed if the 'Mech engages in hand-to-hand combat. The missile-feed system, which passes reloads from the torso storage compartment, is average at best. If damaged, reloads can become lodged in the upper arm, where additional damage has been known to cause detonation, destroying the arm.

Type: **THE-N Thorn**

Equipment		Mass
Internal Structure:	Endo Steel II	1
Engine:	GM 120	4
Walking MP:	6	
Running MP:	9	
Jumping MP:	0	
Heat Sinks:	10	0
Gyro:		2
Cockpit:		3
Armor Factor:	72	4.5

	Internal Structure	Armor Value
Head	3	9
Center Torso	6	8
Center Torso (rear)		4
R/L Torso	5	6
R/L Torso (rear)		4
R/L Arm	3	6
R/L Leg	4	8

Weapons and Ammo:	Location	Critical	
LRM 5	RA	1	2
AMMO LRM 5 (24)	RT	1	1
CASE	RT	1	0.5
Medium Laser	H	1	1
Medium Laser	LA	1	1

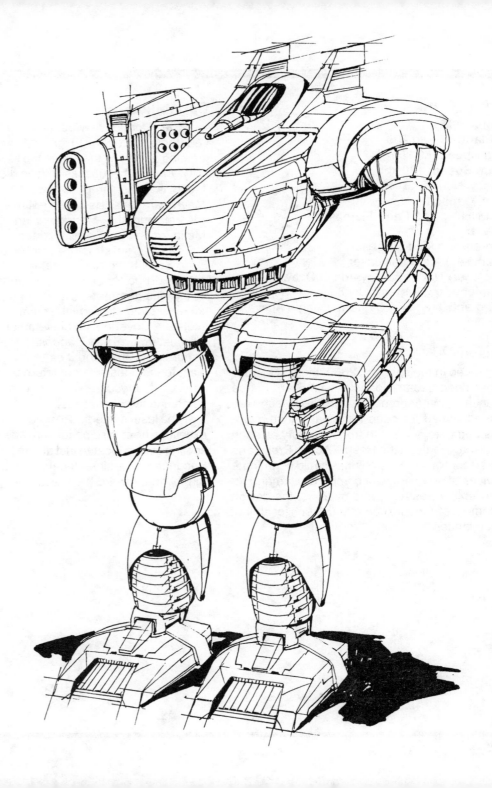

Mass: 25 tons
Chassis: Kell/D
Power Plant: Nissan 200
Cruising Speed: 86 kph
Maximum Speed: 130 kph
Jump Jets: None
   Jump Capacity: None
Armor: Mitchell GA3 Ferro-Fibrous
Armament:
   3 Sorenstein Medium Lasers
   1 Starflash Plus Small Laser
Manufacturer: Diplan 'Mechyards of Ozawa
Communications System: ON-5
Targeting and Tracking System: Beagle Active
   Probe

Overview:

Introduced in the spring of 2660, the quick, agile *Mongoose* soon became popular with Star League Light Lance commanders. Though the 'Mech was originally designed for deep reconnaissance, commanders began to adapt it to front-line duty as soon as they discovered that the Beagle Active Probe and associated central processing units could coordinate the activities of an entire light company. Demand for this new vehicle was high, and by 2668, the design had become the standard command 'Mech for all light and recon lances.

Capabilities:

The *Mongoose* was designed to replace the venerable *Locust*, with ground speed, rather than jumping ability, as the key to the Mech's maneuverability. An instant success with field commanders, the 'Mech is considered an outstanding design. The 'Mech's armament is based entirely on energy weapons, making the *Mongoose* an ideal deep-recon 'Mech, raider, or guerrilla fighter.

The internal structure of the *Mongoose* employs Endo Steel II, an alloy created especially for use in 'Mechs. Endo Steel offers tremendous load-bearing ability plus greater tensile strength, allowing a much lighter skeleton to carry the same weight as a normal skeleton. Covering the skeleton are plates of Ferro-Fibrous Armor. The *Mongoose* carries a heavy load of armor for its size, and it can withstand a direct PPC blast to the chest without internal damage. If necessary, the *Mongoose* can engage medium 'Mechs with some chance of success.

The laser systems are tried and dependable, with excellent heat dissipation provided by the primary cooling collars located just above the 'Mech's elbows. Secondary heat sinks, located in the back of the torso, funnel heat toward the waist. The lasers mounted in the center torso and head are very accurate, employing internal compensators that allow the *Mongoose* to aim precisely when at a full run. The only drawback to the weapon system is the cooling jacket for the center torso laser, which rests on top of the engine compartment and tends to deteriorate rapidly. Replacement is not difficult, but studies show the jacket is virtually useless after 100 firings. The additional heat does not impair the *Mongoose*'s performance, but it makes the cockpit uncomfortable and sometimes interferes with the sensor array.

The Beagle Active Probe, riding within the left shoulder, may be the most important item in the 'Mech. With extended scanner range and a wider scanning-band range, the Beagle can detect and identify vehicles 16 percent faster than any other scanner. Once identified, the target is permanently stored in the Beagle's memory. Should the Beagle encounter the target again, it will remember speed, damage, and even forecast a fighting style to the *Mongoose* pilot. During off hours, the pilot can review any battle on the tactical display, modifying actions with a joystick. The Beagle projects the tactical change and shows the results. This memory device has made the *Mongoose* a highly sought battlefield trainer.

Type: **MON-66 Mongoose**

Equipment			Mass
Internal Structure:	Endo Steel II		1.25
Engine:	Nissan 200		8.5
Walking MP:	8		
Running MP:	12		
Jumping MP:	0		
Heat Sinks:	10		0
Gyro:			2
Cockpit:			3
Armor Factor:	90		5

	Internal Structure	Armor Value
Head	3	9
Center Torso	8	12
Center Torso (rear)		4
R/L Torso	6	10
R/L Torso (rear)		2
R/L Arm	4	8
R/L Leg	6	12

Weapons and Ammo:	Location	Critical	
Medium Laser	RA	1	1
Medium Laser	LA	1	1
Medium Laser	CT	1	1
Small Laser	H	1	0.5
Beagle Probe	LT	2	1.5

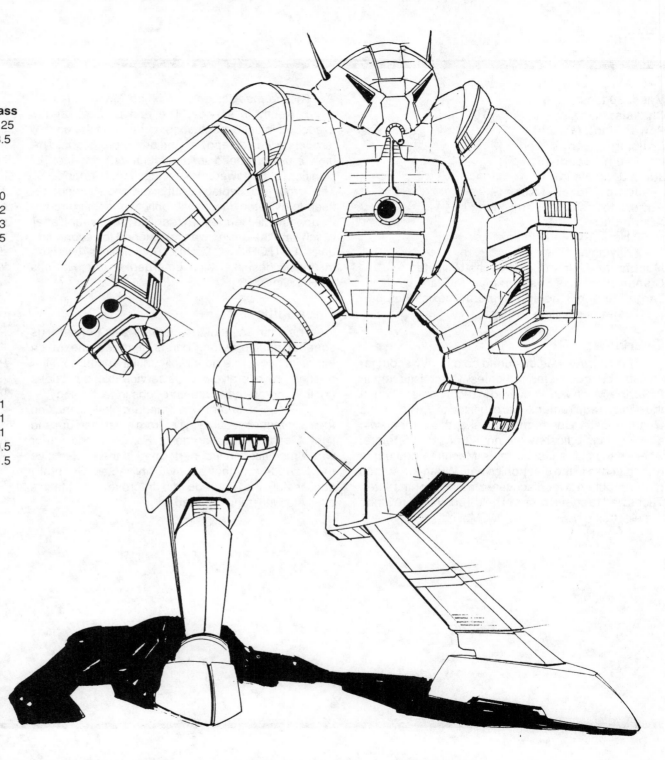

Mass: 30 tons
Chassis: Irian Chassis Class 10
Power Plant: GM 270
Cruising Speed: 97 kph
Maximum Speed: 151 kph
Jump Jets: None
Jump Capacity: None
Armor: Jolassa-328 Ferro-Fibrous
Armament:
　2 Hellion-V Medium Lasers
　1 Olympian Flamer
Manufacturer: Irian BattleMechs Unlimited
Communications System: Irian TelStar
Targeting and Tracking System: Alexis Photon
　Target Acquisition System

Overview:

The *Hermes* was designed as a heavy scout for the Star League Defense Forces. Commissioned in 2632, the 'Mech was delivered in record time. Though the design requirements were fulfilled to the letter, the Quartermaster Command was skeptical of the swift delivery. Line officers were not surprised, therefore, when many of the first *Hermes* 'Mechs turned out to have glitches in the electronics bay. When the source of the problem was discovered many months later, Techs had to spend hours in field-repair time rewiring the electronic bays of the new 'Mechs.

The *Hermes* design called for a 'Mech as fast as any currently in service. The end product greatly exceeded initial expectations, but only at the cost of a severely weak firepower and armor protection. The high cruising speed is desirable, but the lack of significant firepower makes the 'Mech unpopular. The armor is acceptable, but scout pilots cannot get used to a 30-ton 'Mech with only two medium range weapons. The Hermes saw service for 19 years, after which time the design was reassigned to second-line units. [EDITOR'S NOTE: Irian BattleMechs reworked the basic design, which emerged as the *Hermes* HER-2S in 2798.]

Capabilities:

The main asset of the *Hermes* is its tremendous speed. Capable of long bursts of speed, the 'Mech fulfills its scout role admirably until it encounters the enemy. The overall design is serviceable, but it does not incorporate any breakthroughs in technology.

The original armor was standard plating, making the *Hermes* susceptible to fire from most medium and light 'Mechs. The upgrade to Ferro-Fibrous armor was a modification first performed in the field to give the *Hermes* a higher survivability factor. Generally successful, the upgrade did improve the 'Mech's ability to withstand combat.

The single shining piece of equipment on the *Hermes* is the Alexis Photon Target Acquisition System. The Alexis paints the target with light before actually firing either laser. If the Alexis fails to lock onto a high-density target, such as an armored vehicle or 'Mech, the system suspends the order to fire. The fire order is held in a memory buffer until the system acquires a target. If no target is achieved within two seconds, the order is canceled. While the heat buildup in the laser capacitor still has to be dissipated, the system saves wear and tear on the laser focusing apparatus, thus reducing maintenance requirements.

The hand flamer of the *Hermes* is an older design using a fuel mixture rather than tapping into the fusion plant's plasma field. When the weapon is triggered, the upper cylinder, containing a napalm gel, is opened. The gel is forced along pressure hoses toward the nozzle. Instead of exposing the napalm to open flame, the gel mixes with small amounts of specially treated magnesium suspended in water. When the magnesium hits the air, it bursts into flame, igniting the napalm. The system is considered among the safest devised, because the napalm is stored far from the igniting agent. Only a small amount of magnesium is required to ignite the mixture, and so damage to the storage cylinder usually causes only minor damage to the limb. As a further safeguard, ejection racks can jettison the storage cylinders away from the 'Mech.

Type: **HER-1S Hermes**

Equipment		Mass
Internal Structure:	Endo Steel II	1.5
Engine:	GM 270	14.5
Walking MP:	9	
Running MP:	14	
Jumping MP:	0	
Heat Sinks:	10	0
Gyro:		3
Cockpit:		3
Armor Factor:	90	5

	Internal Structure	Armor Value
Head	3	7
Center Torso	10	14
Center Torso (rear)		5
R/L Torso	7	9
R/L Torso (rear)		4
R/L Arm	5	9
R/L Leg	7	10

Weapons and Ammo:	Location	Critical	
Medium Laser	RA	1	1
Flamer	LA	1	1
Medium Laser	CT	1	1

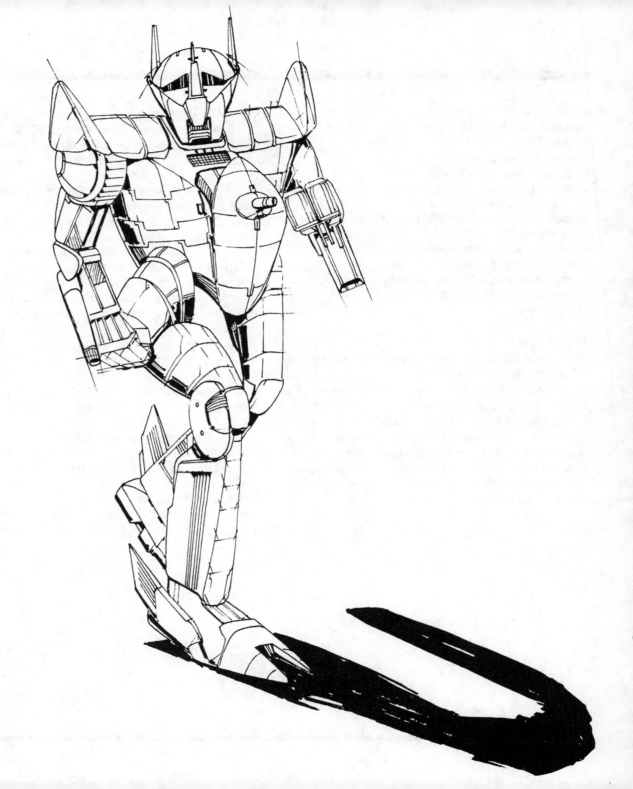

Mass: 30 tons
Chassis: Benztrov 40
Power Plant: GM 270-A
Cruising Speed: 97 kph
Maximum Speed: 151 kph
Jump Jets: None
Jump Capacity: None
Armor: Victory Anchor 2 Ferro-Fibrous
Armament:
1 Newhart Extended-Range Large Laser
Manufacturer: Newhart Industries
Communications System: Field Ranger Sightseer
Targeting and Tracking System: Ranger LAF
Model 2

Overview:

The HSR 200-D *Hussar* is one of the most widely used light recon 'Mechs within the Star League Defense Forces. With a maximum speed of 151 kph, the *Hussar* is a difficult target in a one-on-one fight.

Originally intended to provide close support for infantry units, the 'Mech proved to be so fast that it is a greater asset for reconnaissance. Many *Hussars* began to replace fast scout vehicles, providing superior firepower and greater terrain-handling ability than many scout vehicles.

Capabilities:

The *Hussar* is equipped with an ER large laser, which gives it above-average targeting and range ability with far less maintenance than other similar weapons. Seeing the success of the ER laser, the Star League Quartermaster Command placed an order with Newhart Industries for several hundred other BattleMechs of larger weight and firepower class equipped with the weapon.

The *Hussar* is basically defenseless once it gets within range of other weapons, though it can still charge, kick, and punch. The *Hussar* is occasionally drawn into one-on-one combat with other Battle-Mechs, but it would rarely be the 'Mech of choice for that role.

Another weakness is the overall shortage of armor on the 'Mech. With only 1.5 tons of armor, it lacks the protection of most lighter BattleMechs. Even the early-model *Locust* deployed by the SLDF has twice the armor of an *Hussar*. The *Hussar* is faster, however, and mounts a better weapon. These are delicate tradeoffs in battle, but the net result is that the *Hussar* can disengage by running from a fight against even a lighter BattleMech.

The Ranger communications and targeting systems are also above average, with extended-range capabilities for surveillance missions as well as the ability to jam out most forms of communications.

Thus, several well-placed *Hussars* behind enemy lines can totally disrupt the distribution of orders and troops. A *Hussar* can literally tap into transmissions between enemy BattleMechs 35 kilometers away. The transmission capability of the *Hussar* is also somewhat better than most other SLDF BattleMechs because the *Hussar* is more often reporting on enemy movements and communications, rather than disrupting them.

[Editor's Note: The *Hussar* earned fame for its success in skirting enemy lines and monitoring the enemy. In 2630, during a series of rebellions on the Lyran world of Wotan, near the Dark Nebula, the 51st Hussar Regiment of the XXX Corps was called in at the request of Lyran officials.

Ten *Hussars* known as "The Fingers of Death" dropped far behind enemy lines with little support. Their mission was to disrupt the enemy for as long as possible. During the three-week operation, the 'Mechs destroyed several communications stations and ammunition dumps. Finally, the rebellious locals tracked down several of these raiding *Hussars* and attempted to engage them in combat, only to find the 'Mechs turning tail and running away at staggering speeds.

When the fighting was over, only three of the *Hussars* had been destroyed. The Fingers of Death had proved the combat value of the *Hussar*, and its reputation grew.]

Type: **HSR 200-D Hussar**

Equipment		Mass
Internal Structure:		3
Engine:	GM 270	14.5
Walking MP:	9	
Running MP:	14	
Jumping MP:	0	
Heat Sinks:	10 (20)	0
Gyro:		3
Cockpit:		3
Armor Factor:	27	1.5

	Internal Structure	Armor Value
Head	3	3
Center Torso	10	4
Center Torso (rear)		2
R/L Torso	7	3
R/L Torso (rear)		2
R/L Arm	5	2
R/L Leg	7	2

Weapons and Ammo:	Location	Critical	
ER Large Laser	CT	2	5

STN-3L SENTINEL

Mass: 40 tons
Chassis: Defiant V
Power Plant: Pitban 240
Cruising Speed: 65 kph
Maximum Speed: 97 kph
Jump Jets: None
   Jump Capacity: None
Armor: Valiant Lamellor
Armament:
   1 KWI AC/5 Ultra Autocannon
   1 Defiance B-1A Small Laser
   1 Defiance Streak-2 SRM Launcher
Manufacturer: Defiance Industries
Communications System: StarLink/Benicia Model AS829G
Targeting and Tracking System: Targa-7, Vid-Com-17

Overview:

The STN-3L *Sentinel* is a medium BattleMech, though its 40-ton mass puts it at the low end of its class. Designed to provide battalion-level BattleMech support for infantry and light-armor units, the 'Mech has good maneuverability, long-range hitting power, and an advanced communications system. Equipped with the powerful VidCom-17 and Targa-7 long-range targeting and tracking system, the *Sentinel* is ideal for use in patrols or as a mobile observation post. The 'Mech also carries a StarLink/Benicia Model AS829G communications system. Capable of simultaneous operation on multiple frequencies, this system not only allows the *Sentinel* to monitor closely and to command units operating under it, but also keeps the 'Mech in close contact with rear-area artillery units, calling for fire when needed.

Defiance Industries first produced the *Sentinel* in 2651 for use by House Steiner's private army. The 'Mech appeared one year after the Star League Council had passed an amendment allowing the Council Lords to double their personal household forces. Originally intended for infantry support, the 'Mech soon moved on to the role of guarding military installations and major land holdings of the Steiner family. By the early 28th Century, the design was also in use by the Star League Defense Forces as well as the Davion and Marik private armies.

Capabilities:

The STN-3L's 40-ton frame is powered by the 11.5-ton, Pitban 240 fusion engine, giving the 'Mech a walking speed of 65.4 kph and a top running speed of 97.1 kph. Shortly after the 'Mech's original deployment, concern arose over the choice of the Pitban 240 because of rumors about shielding problems with the Pitban 240s that Defiance Industries was producing under license. After a number of *Sentinel*s were pulled from the field because of chronic overheating, an investigation took place. This investigation found that the heat circulation system was at fault, rather than the engine shielding. The faulty components were replaced in most existing 'Mechs and all later production versions.

The *Sentinel* is well-equipped for combat, carrying a single KWI-5 Ultra Autocannon, a single Defiance Streak-2 SRM launcher, and a single Defiance B-1A Small Laser. Kawabata Weapons Inc. produced the AC/5 Ultra especially for Defiance Industries. The weapon gives the 'Mech good long-range fire capability, with an effective range exceeding that of LRMs and standard AC/5s. Another special feature of this weapon is its ability to fire rounds at double the rate of a standard AC/5. Though this autocannon fire is not as accurate as would be a pair of standard AC/5s, the Ultra does give an equivalent volume of fire.

Unfortunately, besides generating much heat and burning through ammunition supplies very quickly, the extremely high rate of fire has caused some other major problems, particularly on the early STN-3Ls. When fired at its maximum rate, the weapon vibrates violently, causing the internal circuitry in the BattleMech's weapon arm to fail. This often causes a total loss of control of the arm, effectively rendering the AC/5 useless and cutting the *Sentinel*'s combat capabilities almost in half. Though repairs for this problem are simple, the problem keeps the 'Mech out of combat for half an hour or more during repairs.

The current STN-3L has been modified to reduce the chance of disturbances to circuitry. Even these modifications have not solved the problem totally, with an estimated 3 percent chance that the problem will occur whenever the AC/5 Ultra fires at its maximum rate.

The *Sentinel* was not designed to engage in close combat, relying instead on its AC/5 Ultra to hold off enemy units at long range, but it can defend itself if an enemy gets close. Tucked away inside the *Sentinel*'s right torso is its Defiance Streak-2 SRM launcher, linked to a Targa-7 fire control system. This short-range missile system is designed to guarantee a hit against any target onto which the pilot can get a lock. A special feature of this system prevents the weapon from firing at a target when there is no lock-on. This saves ammunition by preventing shots that would miss anyway. Unlike a standard SRM, whose shotgun effect may result in some misses and some hits, the Streak SRM hits with all its missiles. This gives the unit the effective average firepower of the heavier and more wasteful SRM-4 system, but with considerably less variation in damage effects.

When designed, the *Sentinel* was equipped with a Defiance A-1 small laser instead of the B-1A model of current designs. However, the original A-1 small laser was prone to problems after extended field operations, and so the more rugged B-1A was substituted. In 2678, all *Sentinel*s were refitted with the single Defiance B-1A small laser, which is mounted in the right torso, just below the Streak-2 SRM launcher.

Type: **STN-3L Sentinel**

Equipment		Mass
Internal Structure:		4
Engine:	Pitban 240	11.5
Walking MP:	6	
Running MP:	9	
Jumping MP:	0	
Heat Sinks:	10	0
Gyro:		3
Cockpit:		3
Armor Factor:	88	5.5

	Internal Structure	Armor Value
Head	3	9
Center Torso	12	10
Center Torso (rear)		7
R/L Torso	10	8
R/L Torso (rear)		5
R/L Arm	6	8
R/L Leg	10	10

Weapons and Ammo:	Location	Critical	
AC/5 Ultra	LA	5	9
Ammo Ultra (20)	LT	1	1
SRM 2 Streak	RT	1	1.5
Ammo Streak (50)	RT	1	1
Small Laser	RT	1	0.5

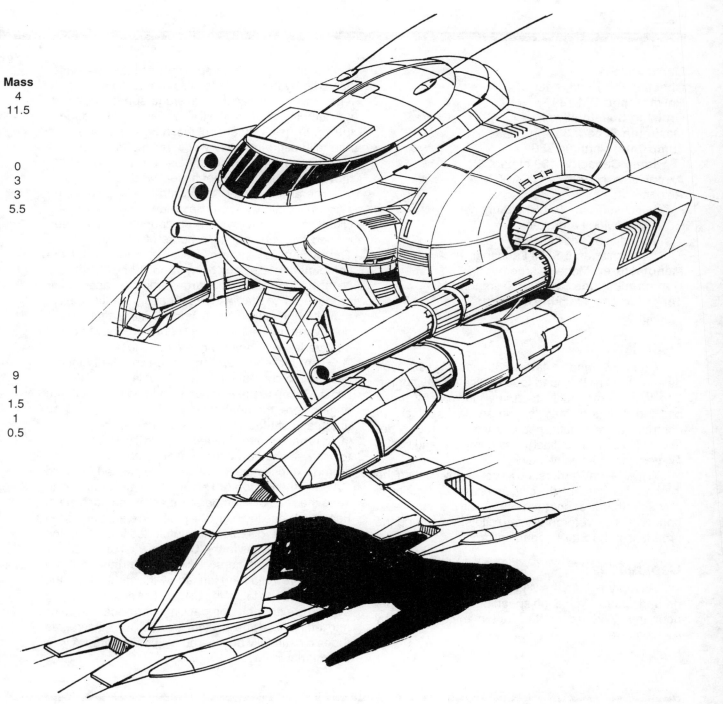

Mass: 45 tons
Chassis: Ost Endo Steel
Power Plant: GM 180
Cruising Speed: 43 kph
Maximum Speed: 65 kph
Jump Jets: Northrup 750
   Jump Capacity: 120 meters
Armor: Kilosh 1000, with CASE
Armament:
   1 Jackson Dart-10 LRM Launcher
   1 Nightwind Large Laser
   2 Starflash Small Lasers
   1 Totschlagen-6 SRM Launcher
Manufacturer: Maltex Corporation
Communications System: Ostmann AMB
Targeting and Tracking System: Scrambler-7
   Series

Overview:

Commissioned in late 2660, the *Wyvern* was developed to fill the need for a dedicated city fighter. The *Wyvern* may fulfill its duties too well, for many pilots dislike the 'Mech's primary tasks of crowd control, garrison duty, security work, or urban defense. These are not flashy assignments, and so the *Wyvern* is not a flashy 'Mech.

A few MechWarriors, however, enjoy piloting the 'Mech. In its element, the city, there are few 'Mechs of any size that it cannot handle, or at the very least harass. These veteran *Wyvern* pilots are among the proudest in the Star League military.

Capabilities:

As a city-fighter, the *Wyvern* does not need much ground speed. With a top speed of 65 kilometers per hour, the *Wyvern* cannot escape many of its foes by running away.

It can, however, jump with considerable ease, powered by the jump jets in its rear torso and upper legs. This combination of average speed and average jumping ability make the *Wyvern* a sitting duck in the open field. When on the attack, the 'Mech is normally used in heavy woods or mountainous terrain, where the ground effects tend to reduce the movement advantages of faster 'Mechs.

The arm-mounted Nightwind Large Laser is the *Wyvern*'s main weapon. Being an older design, the Nightwind's many system components have been refined through countless hours of battlefield tests. The system is extremely reliable, but most of the components are so bulky and heavy that the Nightwind is one of the largest military lasers ever produced. The Starflash Small Lasers cradled next to their bigger cousin were added later, after it was discovered that some of the Nightwind's power could be diverted with no loss of effectiveness.

The Jackson Dart long-range missile launcher has been a constant source of problems for *Wyvern* pilots. Because the weapon is located in front of the engine core, the heat of the engine often causes an automatic shutdown of the system. Normal coolant jackets have proven ineffective, and if a pilot attempts to override shutdown, the heat build-up can lead to an ammo explosion as the reloads are passed from the CASE in the left torso. The only proven solution is to keep the reactor's temperature as low as possible. If heat levels rise too high, the pilot can eject the loaded missiles and disable the autoloader, sealing the remaining missiles in the CASE.

The Totschlagen-6 short-range missiles are much more reliable. Housed in the right torso, the launcher sits on top of the CASE. The entire reloading system is extremely compact, making reloading quick and efficient. If the system should jam, the reload tubes can usually be cleared by jumping the *Wyvern* up and down.

Type: **WVE-5N Wyvern**

Equipment		Mass
Internal Structure:	Endo Steel II	2.25
Engine:	GM 180	7
Walking MP:	4	
Running MP:	6	
Jumping MP:	4	
Heat Sinks:	12	2
Gyro:		2
Cockpit:		3
Armor Factor:	152	9.5

	Internal Structure	Armor Value
Head	3	9
Center Torso	14	20
Center Torso (rear)		7
R/L Torso	11	16
R/L Torso (rear)		6
R/L Arm	7	14
R/L Leg	11	22

Weapons and Ammo:	Location	Critical	
LRM10	CT	2	5
AMMO LRM 10 (12)	LT	1	1
CASE	LT	1	0.5
Large Laser	RA	2	5
Small Laser	RA	1	0.5
Small Laser	RA	1	0.5
SRM 6	RT	2	3
AMMO SRM 6 (15)	RT	1	1
CASE	RT	1	0.5
Jump Jets	LT	1	0.5
Jump Jets	RT	1	0.5
Jump Jets	LL	1	0.5
Jump Jets	RL	1	0.5

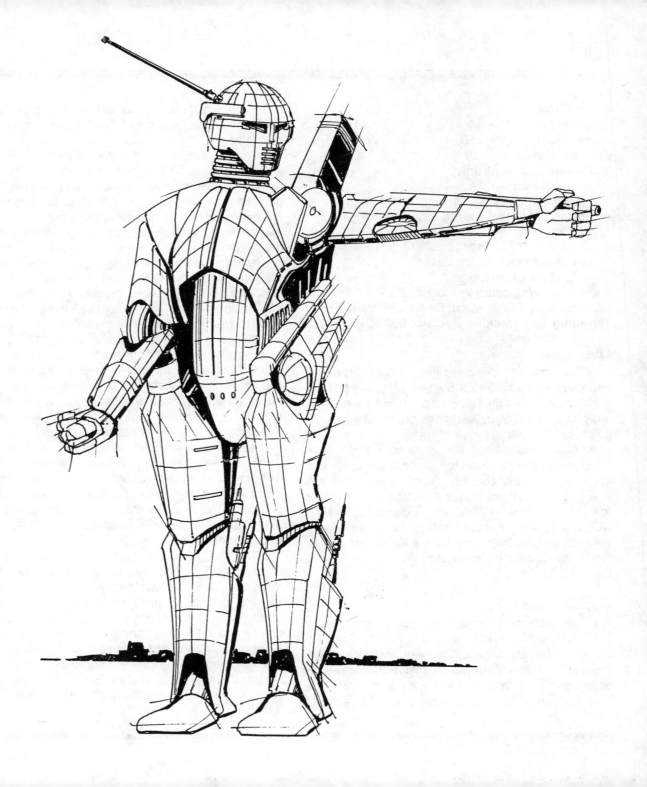

CRB-27 CRAB

Mass: 50 tons
Chassis: Hollis Mark 1A
Power Plant: Magna 250
Cruising Speed: 54 kph
Maximum Speed: 86 kph
Jump Jets: None
    Jump Capacity: None
Armor: Paulina Heavy Ferro-Fibrous
Armament:
    2 RAMTech 1200 Large Lasers
    1 Ceres Arms Medium Laser
    1 ExoStar Small Laser
Manufacturer: Cosara Weaponries
Communications System: Dalban Series K
Targeting and Tracking System: 650 RND

Overview:

The *Crab* was designed to be a medium raider and guerrilla fighter. First built in 2719, fewer than 1,000 of this design have been delivered to their assignments so far. Initial reports on the design were good, but the 'Mech's lack of hands and inability to jump have reduced its usefulness as a raider. The *Crab* possesses good overall speed and can survive for weeks without resupply. All of its weapons are energy-based, which makes the *Crab* slightly hotter to operate than other 'Mechs of its class. [EDITOR'S NOTE: It is likely that the *Crab* would have become the standard medium 'Mech of the SLDF had events not forced General Kerensky and his loyalists to leave the Inner Sphere.]

Capabilities:

The *Crab* contains little new technology. Except for the targeting system and the communications equipment, every major component on the *Crab* has been proven on another 'Mech design. Techs dream of assignment to a *Crab*, because the maintenance time is less than half that for other 'Mechs in its class.

A *Crab* Walk is synonymous with easy duty. Only the communications equipment gives the Techs any problems.

The Dalban Series K communications network was designed to be fully self-contained. The system houses seven microprocessors, each capable of performing its own special duty as well as duplicating the operations of the other six. More than a communication systems, the Dalban network can identitify the 'Mech's exact location on the world and locations of any known units on the planet. The system keeps the information current by monitoring all radio frequencies and short-wave bands. When operating behind enemy lines, the system can forecast enemy troop movements, differentiating between suspected positions and known positions, and project a path for arriving at any goal. Though not foolproof, the system does give the pilot an excellent recon report prior to his patrol. Unfortunately, the system is difficult to maintain. Damage to one of the processors normally requires its complete removal. The system redundancy was absolutely necessary to keep the system on line during combat.

The *Crab*'s armor protection is generally good. The arms and legs are especially well-protected, with Ferro-Fibrous Armor used throughout. Its weakest areas of protection are the left and right torsos, but even those areas can withstand a direct PPC blast without a breach.

The 'Mech's weapons systems are functional, but uninspired. The large lasers are a matched set, housed in the claws and forearms of each arm. They provide an excellent arc of fire but are easily damaged during hand-to-hand fighting. Pilots have a tendency to use the huge weapons as clubs, knocking the focusing mirrors out of alignment and rendering the laser inoperable. Though the adjustment is easy to perform, it requires several minutes outside the cockpit with the pilot's head buried in the elbow of the 'Mech.

To provide a secondary line of defense, a medium Ceres Arms laser and ExoStar small laser were added in the center torso and head, respectively. The medium laser is well-protected from the engine, and heat sinks allow an unrestricted flow of heat through the center torso and out of the back. The head-mounted small laser is normally used only as a last resort. Ineffective at long ranges, it is best used against soft targets, such as infantry and rioting civilians. The cockpit is well-insulated from the heat of the engine and the small laser. Pilots appreciate the relative comfort of piloting a *Crab*.

The 'Mech's ejection seat varies from the standard design. The pilot has two methods of escape. If an explosion is imminent, the top hatch is blown back and the seat is jettisoned through the roof of the 'Mech. Seat thrusters stabilize the descent to a controlled fall, and the pilot lands roughly 200 meters from his machine. If no explosion is likely, the seat is rotated 90 degrees and fired out the back. The pilot will land 20 to 50 meters from his 'Mech after a much shorter and gentler ride.

Type: **CRB-27 Crab**

Equipment		Mass
Internal Structure:		5
Engine:	Magna 250	12.5
Walking MP:	5	
Running MP:	8	
Jumping MP:	0	
Heat Sinks:	16	6
Gyro:		3
Cockpit:		3
Armor Factor:	161	9

	Internal Structure	Armor Value
Head	3	9
Center Torso	16	20
Center Torso (rear)		8
R/L Torso	12	16
R/L Torso (rear)		6
R/L Arm	8	16
R/L Leg	12	24

Weapons and Ammo:	Location	Critical	
Large Laser	LA	2	5
Large Laser	RA	2	5
Medium Laser	CT	1	1
Small Laser	H	1	0.5

Mass: 55 tons
Chassis: Technicron-1
Power Plant: Core Tek 275
Cruising Speed: 54 kph
Maximum Speed: 86 kph
Jump Jets: None
   Jump Capacity: None
Armor: Leopard V Ferro-Fibrous
Armament:
   1 Narc Missile Beacon
   1 Holly-5 LRM Launcher
   2 HoverTec-6 SRM Launchers
   2 Magna Medium Lasers
Manufacturer: General Mechanics
Communications System: OmniComm 3
Targeting and Tracking System: Starbeam 3000

Overview:

The *Kintaro* is a rare example of a 'Mech designed around a weapons system, the Narc Missile Beacon. The 'Mech was to incorporate the Narc system, with ample firepower to take advantage of any hit achieved by the Narc pods. The 'Mech would be mainly an offensive weapon, able to work with a variety of other 'Mechs, but also required to carry maximum armor. The primary mission of the new 'Mech was to deliver the Narc pods to the target and let its lancemates provide the punishment. In 2587, the Quartermaster Command approved the General Mechanics *Kintaro* design.

Primarily a missile-carrier, the *Kintaro* packs a considerable punch. It is not a raider, however. Though it carries ample supplies for a single engagement, it is almost constantly in need of resupply. As any fight wears on, the effectiveness of the *Kintaro* decreases geometrically. Once the Narc Pods are gone, the *Kintaro* usually begins to look for a way out of the fighting.

Capabilities:

Rarely has the introduction of a single weapon system caused as much stir as the unveiling of the Narc Missile Beacon. Introduced in 2587, the Narc and the *Kintaro* were a matched set. The Narc system was a radically new way to activate a missile's target-acquisition computer. Special missiles, called pods, were fitted with powerful homing beacons behind a magnetic head. If a hit was achieved, the Narc Pod would emit a clear homing signal for all Narc-equipped missile systems in the area. Target lock-on was virtually guaranteed with the Narc in place.

The *Kintaro* mounts the Narc Missile Beacon in the heavily protected center torso, directly over the engine. Thickly shielded, the internal workings of the *Kintaro* mesh completely with the Narc. The Narc Pods are housed in the right torso and fed to the firing system by a sophisticated autoloader. The overall system is very reliable, but somewhat spread out. Although protected by tons of Ferro-Fibrous armor, the Narc System is vulnerable to any breach in the upper torso. The launcher is, however, of fairly standard design and can easily be replaced.

The twin HoverTec short-range missile launchers, while similar in effect, are totally different in design. The torso-mounted system is fairly standard. Very compact, the reloads sit next to the launcher, providing an excellent rate of fire and a high reliability rating. The left-arm system, however, is a technician's nightmare. Installed to provide a wider arc of fire, the arm-mounted autoloader requires daily maintenance. The lower arm houses both the Holly-5 long-range missile launcher and one of the HoverTech-6 SRMs. The reloads, however, are stored in the left torso. When reloading occurs, the missiles travel down the upper arm into the launch tubes. Reloading requires three seconds, during which time the arm must remain nearly motionless. The system automatically locks the arm in place for the moment

required, but any movement in the system invariably causes a jam in the upper arm. The time required to clear the jam varies greatly, but usually takes at least an hour.

The Holly-5 LRM uses the same principle and works like a charm. Missiles are stored in the torso and fed through the upper arm to the launcher on the forearm. When jamming occurs, it is in the storage area, prior to the missile's entry into the loading tube, but jamming is rare. Why the two systems show such differences in performance is not known.

The twin medium lasers mounted on the right arm are there more for the pilot's peace of mind than to fight the enemy. It is a comfort to a MechWarrior if he always has something to fall back on when times get tough. The lasers provide a good arc of fire and work well as a supplement to the missile system.

Type: **KTO-19 Kintaro**

Equipment		Mass
Internal Structure:		5.5
Engine:	Core Tek 275	15.5
Walking MP:	5	
Running MP:	8	
Jumping MP:	0	
Heat Sinks:	10	0
Gyro:		3
Cockpit:		3
Armor Factor:	179	10

	Internal Structure	Armor Value
Head	3	9
Center Torso	18	26
Center Torso (rear)		10
R/L Torso	13	18
R/L Torso (rear)		8
R/L Arm	9	18
R/L Leg	13	23

Weapons and Ammo:	Location	Critical	
Narc Beacon	CT	2	3
Narc Pods-6	RT	1	2
LRM 5	LA	1	2
AMMO LRM 5 (24)	LT	1	1
SRM 6	LA	2	3
AMMO SRM 6 (15)	LT	1	1
SRM 6	RT	2	3
AMMO SRM 6 (15)	RT	1	1
Medium Laser	RA	1	1
Medium Laser	RA	1	1

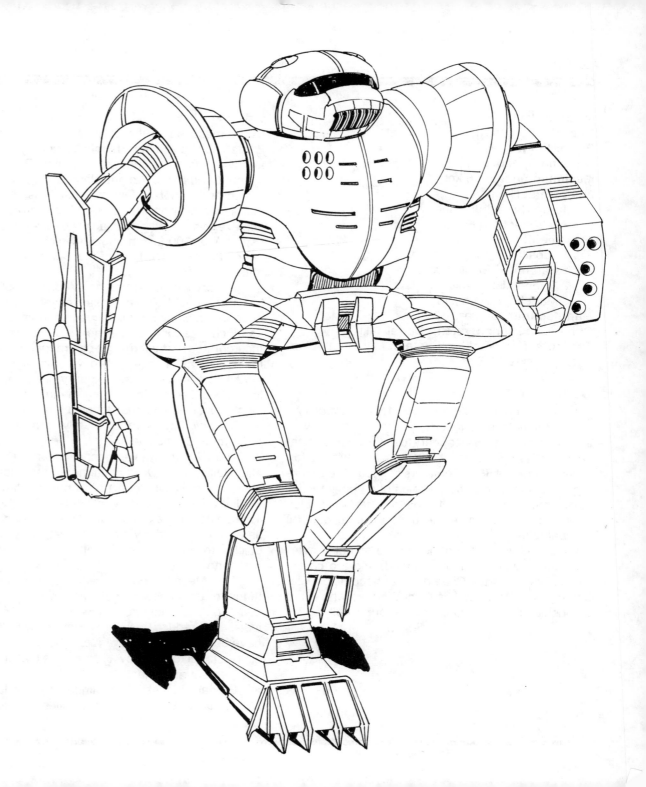

Mass: 60 tons
Chassis: Bergan XI
Power Plant: Vlar 300
Cruising Speed: 54 kph
Maximum Speed: 86 kph
Jump Jets: None
   Jump Capacity: None
Armor: 2/Star Slab Ferro-Fibrous
Armament:
   1 Lubalin LB 10-X Autocannon
   1 Harpoon-6 SRM Launcher
   2 Magna MkII Medium Lasers
   2 Martell Small Lasers
Manufacturer: Bergan Industries
Communications System: Garret T-11C
Targeting and Tracking System: Mercury-IV plus
   Artemis IV FCS

Overview:

Introduced in 2602, the CHP-1N *Champion* is a heavy BattleMech designed to be fast and maneuverable, with an array of weaponry to give it good combat flexibility. Weighing in at 60 tons and with a top running speed of 86.4 kilometers per hour, the *Champion* was intended to fill the roles of a heavy reconnaissance and strike BattleMech. The 'Mech also often serves with main-line units in more general combat roles.

Many have criticized the vehicle as being over-engined, oversized, under-gunned, and too costly. Despite its critics, the *Champion* has become popular among its pilots as well as MechWarriors who serve alongside the *Champion*, for it performs well.

Capabilities:

Its mass makes the CHP-1N *Champion* a heavy BattleMech, but it has feeble weaponry and light armor for this class. Though many other BattleMechs in the *Champion*'s weight class are more heavily armed and armored, few can match its speed and maneuverability and, thus, its higher survival rate. To achieve this speed advantage, however, the 'Mech uses a Vlar 300 fusion engine, which itself masses nearly 20 tons, one-third of the *Champion*'s overall mass.

Critics claim that a medium 'Mech in the 50- to 55-ton range could obtain similar movement performance with a smaller engine, leaving room for almost as much weaponry and armor. Indeed, Earthwerks Incorporated bid for the same contract with a proposal for the GRF-3N, a modified version of its 55-ton *Griffin*, to achieve the same performance at notably less cost. Bergan Industries, manufacturer of the highly successful *Locust*, lobbied so intensively that its *Champion* proposal ultimately won out with an order for 200 machines.

The *Champion*'s weaponry consists of one Lubalin Ballistics 10-X autocannon, one Harpoon-6 short-range missile launcher, a pair of Magna MkII Medium Lasers, and two Martell Small Lasers. Though carrying extra ammunition, the 'Mech sometimes must withdraw from combat early or close quickly to engage targets with its SRM and laser weaponry.

The 'Mech's greatest weakness may be that it tends to run somewhat hot when involved in heavy combat, due mostly to the low-efficiency heat sinks installed to reduce the overall cost. Many SLDF units have begun to remove the *Champion*'s original heat sinks for replacement by a newer type that dissipates 100 percent more heat.

Bergan Industries continues to produce the *Champion* at two of its 'Mech facilities on New Earth.

Type: **CHP-1N Champion**

Equipment			Mass
Internal Structure:			6
Engine:	Vlar 300		19
Walking MP:	5		
Running MP:	8		
Jumping MP:	0		
Heat Sinks:	10		0
Gyro:			3
Cockpit:			3
Armor Factor:	143		8

	Internal Structure	Armor Value	
Head	3	9	
Center Torso	20	24	
Center Torso (rear)		8	
R/L Torso	14	18	
R/L Torso (rear)		6	
R/L Arm	10	12	
R/L Leg	14	15	

Weapons and Ammo:	Location	Critical	
LB 10-X	RT	6	11
Ammo LB 10-X(20)	RT	2	2
SRM 6	LT	2	3
AMMO SRM 6 (15)	LT	1	1
Artemis IV FCS	CT	1	1
Medium Laser	LT	1	1
Medium Laser	LT	1	1
Small Laser	CT	1	0.5
Small Laser	CT	1	0.5

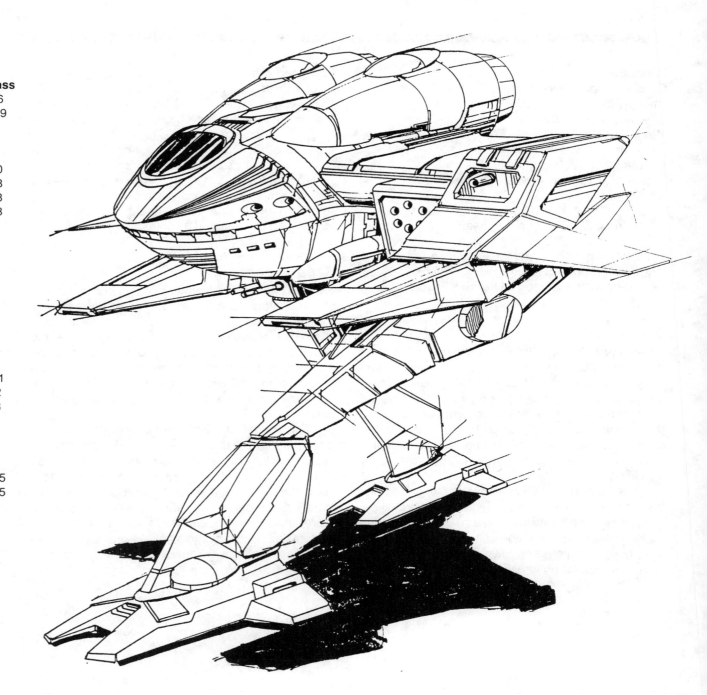

Mass: 60 tons
Chassis: MangoTech 500 SJ (Spiral Jection)
Power Plant: Hermes 360XL
Cruising Speed: 65 kph
Maximum Speed: 97 kph
Jump Jets: None
   Jump Capacity: None
Armor: PanzerSlab Type 5
Armament:
   1 Kinslaughter PPC
   2 Krupp Model 32 Large Lasers
   1 Krupp Model 2 Medium Laser
Manufacturer: Krupp Stellar Technologies Inc.
Communications System: Krupp-COMM 500
Targeting and Tracking System: KBC Starsight
   Model

Overview:

In 2581, Krupp Stellar Technologies Inc. was awarded a Star League contract to produce a medium combat BattleMech. Though well-known for their weapons and battle computers, Krupp had yet to produce a 'Mech for the Star League military. Thus did their engineers outdo themselves in the effort to perfect their design, which they named the *Lancelot*, and which came in slightly overweight, in the heavy classification.

The Star League Quartermaster Command had laid down relatively simple criteria for the prototype. They asked for a 'Mech that could operate with limited dependency on ammunition or support and that was fast enough for mobile operation. In addition to these qualities, they asked for sufficient firepower to make the 'Mech a viable force in combat.

Faced with these demands, the design staff at Krupp Stellar equipped the *Lancelot* with the Hermes 360XL engine system. The XL is a rare engine series that produces extended output and endurance and weighs less than conventional fusion plants.

During trial runs on Soul during the spring of 2581, the Star League officials were impressed with the *Lancelot*'s displays of firepower and speed. Though Krupp Stellar Technologies was a relatively small firm and the *Lancelot* would be its first Battle-Mech, the SLDF granted a contract for an initial order of 250 'Mechs.

Capabilities:

The *Lancelot* is a superior design from a number of standpoints. Its most important design feature is the Hermes 360XL power plant. Subtle alterations in shielding placement and core positioning allowed the engine's designers to drop tons from the weight of the power plant. This allowed the addition of several more heat sinks in the 'Mech's center torso, giving it superior heat-venting capability. Designers also added armor to critical locations.

The Krupp KBC battle computer had long been a standard that other firms used. In the *Lancelot*, the computer was programmed to monitor a wider range of input to match the capabilities of the engine and the computer. Thus, a *Lancelot* pilot can check such factors as current armor status and skin temperature. More important, the *Lancelot*'s internal monitoring systems do not inhibit the other abilities of the Battle-Mech in a fighting environment.

The *Lancelot*'s targeting and tracking system, the Krupp KBC Starsight Model 3, is a perfect example of a manufacturer taking full advantage of a system's abilities. In a fierce battlefield situation, where hundreds of projectiles can fill the air in a matter of seconds, the Starsight singles out those 'Mechs targeting the *Lancelot*, highlighting them for immediate attention. Not only is this a strong advantage in a large-scale battle, but the Model 3 also instantly identifies the most serious threat. Most targeting systems can monitor up to 20 different targets simultaneously, but the Starsight Model 3 can manage up to 50, depending on the situation.

The *Lancelot*'s profile is lean compared to most 'Mechs of the same production era. There are subtle curves in the contour of the PanzerSlab Type 5 Armor plates where many 'Mechs show corners and blunt edges. This tends to give the LNC 25-01 a narrower silhouette for enemy BattleMechs to target and hit.

The *Lancelot*'s main weaponry is not overly impressive for a 'Mech of its weight, however. The Kinslaughter PPC is well-known for its difficulties in insulation. If not properly maintained, it will begin to generate more heat than most weapons of the same type, making preventive maintenance more of a priority than on other 'Mechs. The *Lancelot*'s other weapons are good. The Krupp Model 32 Large Lasers (known as "Fur Burners" among MechWarriors who use and favor them) are renowned for their performance, especially when linked with the capabilities of a KBC Battle Computer. The *Lancelot* also mounts a Krupp Model 12 Medium Laser in its center torso.

Type: **LNC 25-01 Lancelot**

Equipment		Mass
Internal Structure:		6
Engine:	Hermes 360XL	16.5
Walking MP:	6	
Running MP:	9	
Jumping MP:	0	
Heat Sinks:	13 (26)	3
Gyro:		4
Cockpit:		3
Armor Factor:	152	9.5

	Internal Structure	Armor Value
Head	3	7
Center Torso	20	21
Center Torso (rear)		16
R/L Torso	14	16
R/L Torso (rear)		10
R/L Arm	10	14
R/L Leg	14	14

Weapons and Ammo:	Location	Critical	
PPC	RT	3	7
Large Laser	RA	2	5
Large Laser	LA	2	5
Medium Laser	CT	1	1

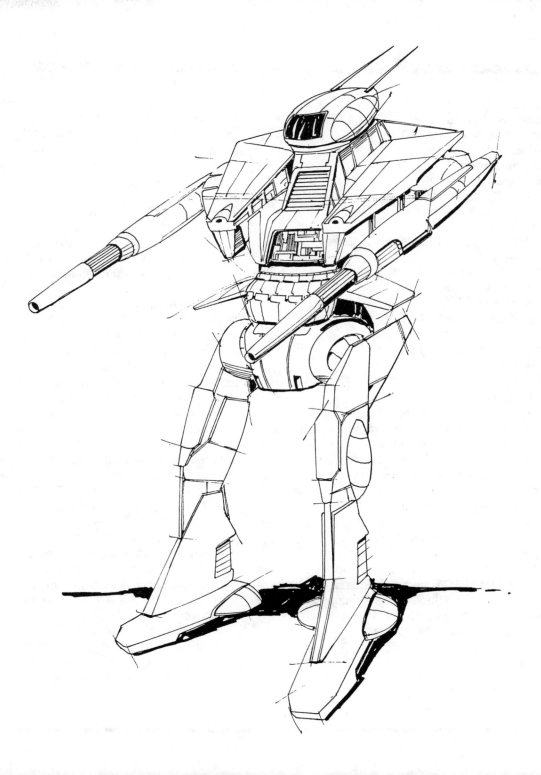

Mass: 65 tons
Chassis: SL Special
Power Plant: Magna 390XL
Cruising Speed: 65 kph
Maximum Speed: 97 kph
Jump Jets: Chevron II
  Jump Capacity: 180 meters
Armor: Fibrolyte Armorscale
Armament:
  4 Averell Highpoint Medium Lasers
  1 Deadeye-10 LRM Launcher
  1 Buzzsaw Anti-Missile System
  1 Dinatech Mark III Small Laser
Manufacturer: General Systems
Communications System: AR-12 Sheathed
  Directional Beacon
Targeting and Tracking System: DLK Type Phased
  Array Sensors

Overview:

'Mechs are designed for specialized purposes, such as scouting on a desert planet or headquarters jamming. One of these in the era of specialization is the *Exterminator*, whose sole function is to target specific command 'Mechs and destroy them.

After successful field tests and practice exercises, the 'Mech finally went on active status in 2630, and it became popular with 'Mech units because of its sleek appearance and state-of-the-art battle systems. Being assigned to one of the most dangerous specialized missions, the *Exterminator* is equipped with the latest in ECM and null signature devices. It was also the first 'Mech to be equipped with the Chameleon Light Polarization Shield, which greatly reduced its chance of being seen.

[EDITOR'S NOTE: In spite of its extensive abilities, or perhaps because of them, the *Exterminator* did not survive the First Succession War. The various Successor State armies began to train specialized 'Mech lances purely to seek out and destroy *Exterminator*s.]

Capabilities:

The EXT-4D *Exterminator* design was conceived to be an efficient 'Mech assigned to carry out a specific mission. Accordingly, all of its systems were constructed and integrated with this single mission in mind.

First and foremost, the newly designed Magna 390XL engine offers vastly improved power-to-weight ratio. This gives the 65-ton *Exterminator* maneuverability similar to that of many 20-ton scout 'Mechs. The newly designed Chevron II jump jets offer even more latitude to the *Exterminator*'s mode of operations.

Of special importance to the *Exterminator*'s mission are its electronic countermeasure and null signature systems, many of which have subsequently been incorporated into other 'Mech designs as well. One of the most important stealth systems aboard the 'Mech are its heat baffles. When the *Exterminator* is in stealth mode, all the heat generated by normal operations, such as walking, is shunted out through a series of heat baffles in the 'Mech's feet. If the pilot is cautious, this waste heat is released into the ground and then dissipated into the surrounding area. Only direct heat sensors at close range can detect these warm areas of ground that are the *Exterminator*'s footprints. When combined with the Phased Array Sensor System, the Sheathed Directional Communication Beacon, and the Chameleon Light Polarization Shield, the heat dissipaters allow the *Exterminator* to cover great distances with little chance of discovery.

The *Exterminator* is protected with standard Fibrolyte Armorscale but with improved anti-laser ablatives added to the first four layers. This gives the 'Mech an intense silver sheen when not screened, which must be kept clean to ensure efficiency of the reflective laser defense.

The *Exterminator*'s weapons array is designed with close-in combat in mind because the 'Mech must infiltrate enemy positions and rapidly eliminate key commanders and their 'Mechs, then return to friendly lines. The two Averell Highpoint medium lasers on each of the 'Mech's forearms help it achieve this objective.

The EXT-4D is also equipped with a Deadeye LRM-10 Rack mounted on the upper central torso. Its only other weapons are a small, head-mounted Dinatech Mark III small laser and the Buzzsaw Anti-Missile System mounted on the right shoulder. This weapon can throw a stream of shells in the path of incoming missiles, with a good chance of destroying them before they hit the *Exterminator*. The system's automatic tracking and firing component frees up the 'Mech pilot for other matters while the Buzzsaw takes care of air defense.

Because of its extremely specialized mission, the *Exterminator* is not normally placed in standard 'Mech lance units. Instead, they are attached to Regimental Headquarters or higher, then assigned to smaller echelon units as needed. If a regiment is lucky, it might have more than one of these 'Mechs assigned to it. It is not unusual for Brigade or Divisional Headquarters to pull *Exterminator*s away from their assigned regiments for missions elsewhere within the Divisional Area.

When not on a mission, Exterminators are assigned directly to a unit's Headquarters Lance, making it a temporary fifth member.

Type: EXT-4D Exterminator

Equipment		Mass
Internal Structure:		6.5
Engine:	Magna 390XL	23
Walking MP:	6	
Running MP:	9	
Jumping MP:	6	
Heat Sinks:	10 [20]	0
Gyro:		4
Cockpit:		3
Armor Factor:	168	10.5

	Internal Structure	Armor Value
Head	3	9
Center Torso	21	21
Center Torso (rear)		8
R/L Torso	15	20
R/L Torso (rear)		8
R/L Arm	10	18
R/L Leg	15	19

Weapons and Ammo:	Location	Critical	
LRM10	CT	2	5
AMMO LRM 10 (12)	CT	1	1
Medium Laser	RA	1	1
Medium Laser	RA	1	1
Medium Laser	LA	1	1
Medium Laser	LA	1	1
Small Laser	H	1	0.5
Anti-Missile	RT	1	0.5
Anti-Missile Ammo (12)	RT	1	1
Jump Jets	RT	3	3
Jump Jets	LT	3	3

BMB-12D BOMBARDIER

Mass: 65 tons
Chassis: KetoBond
Power Plant: Vox 325XL
Cruising Speed: 54 kph
Maximum Speed: 86 kph
Jump Jets: None
Jump Capacity: None
Armor: Choutaka Armorscale, Ltd., with CASE
Armament:
2 Delphinius-20 LRM Launchers
1 Arrowlite-4 SRM Launcher
1 Buzzsaw Anti-Missile System
Manufacturer: Wakazashi Enterprises
Communications System: Neil 9000
Targeting and Tracking System: DLK Type Phased
Array Sensors

Overview:

The *Bombardier* 'Mech was developed as part of a trend toward specialized 'Mechs. Wakazashi Enterprises proposed its design for an "artillery 'Mech" in 2735.

The idea was to produce a 'Mech that could replace mechanized mobile units such as wheeled or tracked artillery vehicles for rear-area artillery support. Vehicles often fell behind a BattleMech advance, and other times an enemy 'Mech penetration of the front lines overran artillery pieces because of their comparative lack of mobility.

The *Bombardier* was designed to carry special missile racks that could fire diverse missile types, all of them superior to simple artillery fire tube ordnance. Some of the missile types developed included the Swarm Missile and the Thunder Missile. The Swarm Missile was designed to be fired indirectly at a designated target identified by a forward observer/spotter (either in another 'Mech or not). Each Swarm Missile contains 100 submunitions, which separate when the

missile reaches the target area. A barrage of 20 such missiles from half of the *Bombardier*'s long-range racks can devastate a large area. Thunder Missiles are similar in design to Swarm Missiles, except that they contain 5 mines that spread out in the path of advancing BattleMechs. These mines have enough explosive force to damage the legs of many 'Mechs. The *Bombardier* can carry other missile types in different combat situations.

[EDITOR'S NOTE: More than 800 *Bombardier*s were put into service with the Star League Defense Forces. They passed every test and field exercise with honors, continually proving vehicle-borne artillery to be no match for the *Bombardier*. Just before the fall of the Star League, there was even talk of disbanding the artillery arm of the army as soon as there were enough operational *Bombardier*s to replace the mobile artillery throughout the Inner Sphere. These plans never materialized, however.

Despite years of tests and wargame exercises, the *Bombardier* revealed some problems in actual extended-combat situations. Foremost among these was the rapid expenditure of its specialized missile armaments. Stores of Bombardier Artillery Missiles dried up on many planets after no more than three days of battle. With space traffic disrupted and munitions factories being destroyed daily all around the Successor States, resupply was haphazard at best.

As the First Succession War dragged on, more and more *Bombardier*s were ordered into front-line lances to act as close support, just as were the old *Archer*s. Not designed for a slugging match, the *Bombardier* quickly became the 'Mech type with the most losses on the battlefield. As spare parts and replacements dried up, a number of damaged *Bombardier*s were cannibalized to keep other support 'Mechs running. *Bombardier* parts and equipment can be seen on hybrid 'Mechs to this day.

By the beginning of the Second Succession War, only a handful of *Bombardier*s remained in operation. Most of these were deployed guarding the last few munitions factories capable of constructing the *Bombardier*'s specialized artillery missiles. When leaving these factory planets for a special operation, *Bombardier*s were always followed by wheeled or tracked supply vehicles carrying what was intended as ample additional missile ammunition. It is ironic that at the end of the *Bombardier*'s active role, it operated only with the support of the very type of vehicle it was designed to replace.]

Capabilities:

The BMB-12D *Bombardier* is efficient in its assigned role. Its Vox 325XL power plant allows it to stay within support range of advancing 'Mech units. This extra speed also allows it to change its position to avoid counter battery fire.

The two Delphinius Long Range Missile 20-racks can launch myriad types of missiles. At shorter range, the Arrowlite SRMs can be used. The *Bombardier*'s only defensive armament is the Buzzsaw Anti-Missile System, designed to defend the 'Mech against missile fire.

The *Bombardier*'s armor is considered substantial for its assigned role. It has as much armor as its larger cousin, the *Archer*, but on a smaller chassis. Even in battlefield conditions, the armor of the BMB-12D is sufficient. The 'Mech is also equipped with CASE.

*Bombardier*s are usually grouped into their own support lance, normally assigned to the Headquarters Company of a 'Mech regiment. No regiment ever has more than a four-*Bombardier* lance, but this is not enough artillery support for an entire regiment, despite the 'Mech's efficient armament. Normal artillery vehicle batteries have never been eliminated from any unit's table of organization.

Type: **BMB-12D Bombardier**

Equipment		Mass
Internal Structure:		6.5
Engine:	Vox 325 XL	11.75
Walking MP:	5	
Running MP:	8	
Jumping MP:	0	
Heat Sinks:	10 [20]	0
Gyro:		4
Cockpit:		3
Armor Factor:	200	12.5

	Internal Structure	Armor Value
Head	3	9
Center Torso	21	24
Center Torso (rear)		15
R/L Torso	15	20
R/L Torso (rear)		10
R/L Arm	10	20
R/L Leg	15	26

Weapons and Ammo:	Location	Critical	
LRM 20	RT	5	10
LRM 20	LT	5	10
AMMO LRM 20 (12)	RT	2	2
CASE	RT	1	0.5
SRM 4	RA	1	2
AMMO SRM 4 (25)	RA	1	1
Anti-Missile	CT	1	0.5
Anti-Missile Ammo (12)	CT	1	1

Mass: 70 tons
Chassis: Crucis-I
Power Plant: Vox 280
Cruising Speed: 43 kph
Maximum Speed: 65 kph
Jump Jets: Anderson 398
  Jump Capacity: 120 meters
Armor: Ulston Prime Ferro-Fibrous, with CASE
Armament:
  1 Sunglow Large Laser
  1 Coventry-6 SRM Launcher
  4 ExoStar II Medium Lasers
Manufacturer: Newhart Industries
Communications System: StarLink 955G
Targeting and Tracking System: Pulsar Tri-X

Overview:

The *Guillotine* is a venerable design. Commissioned in 2499, the 'Mech has seen action in every major Star League Defense Forces action. The *Guillotine* was the standard heavy 'Mech for generations, working with companies of *Griffins* to provide heavy firepower. As time passed, however, technological improvements made bigger and bigger 'Mechs possible. Though still a capable design, the *Guillotine* is no longer as common as in ages past.

When heavier assault 'Mechs came into existence, the *Guillotine*'s role changed from that of line trooper to raider. Few of the newer, heavier 'Mechs could match the maneuverability and staying power of the *Guillotine*, which is why it remained in production, despite being under-armed compared to other 'Mechs.

Capabilities:

New *Guillotine* pilots are often surprised by the 'Mech's nimbleness. Despite carrying twelve tons of armor, the 'Mech moves with considerable ease. The four jump jet nozzles can propel the *Guillotine* 120 meters and allow it to land with bone-crushing force. The pilot's command chair is specially designed to compensate for the force of these landings.

The *Guillotine*'s primary weapon is the left-arm-mounted Sunglow Large Laser, backed up by four ExoStar II Medium Lasers, one on each side of the torso and two mounted on the right arm. These energy weapons give the 'Mech a good cutting force, but they do not give the 'Mech the punch of other heavy 'Mechs. Though the Sunglow is a dependable weapon, occasional problems may arise with the power cables leading from the chest to the arm. As the cables pass through the shoulder, they run near the surface of the underarm and may bind when the 'Mech raises its left arm over its head. Experienced pilots know to lower the arm and try again, but rookies sometimes attempt to force the line, snapping the feeds in the process and rendering the 'Mech's most potent weapon inoperable. The repair is also costly and time-consuming, as each severed cable must be completely rerun from chest to forearm.

When originally installed, the medium lasers were considered the cutting edge of technology, though now they are quite common. Each laser has two components, the power-supply unit in the heart of the *Guillotine* and the fire-control system in the barrel. Eight pairs of fiber-optic cables carry power to the firing mechanism. The system has an excellent combat survival rate because the bulky power supply, normally the first casualty, is well-hidden.

The secondary weapon system is the Coventry-6 short-range missile system and CASE. Located in the center torso, the SRM provides back-up armament. As with many add-ons, the system had several annoying glitches, most of which were repaired early in the 'Mech's career. Some, however, persist to this day. The most serious is the arming regulator. For unknown reasons, the system sometimes fails to arm missiles five and six. An erratic problem, the cause of the failure has never been traced, despite a complete redesign of the arming system and countless hours of computer diagnoses. Because the occurrence of the problem is irregular, it has not stopped the production of the *Guillotine*, nor has it significantly decreased its usefulness.

The Cellular Ammunition Storage Equipment protects the *Guillotine*'s internal systems, should the stored missiles detonate. Lining the missile storage compartment with additional Ferro-Fibrous plating minimizes damage to other components.

Type: **GLT-3N Guillotine**

Equipment		Mass
Internal Structure:	Endo Steel II	3.5
Engine:	Vox 280	16
Walking MP:	4	
Running MP:	6	
Jumping MP:	4	
Heat Sinks:	25	15
Gyro:		3
Cockpit:		3
Armor Factor:	192	12

	Internal Structure	Armor Value
Head	3	9
Center Torso	22	27
Center Torso (rear)		2
R/L Torso	15	22
R/L Torso (rear)		8
R/L Arm	11	20
R/L Leg	15	22

Weapons and Ammo:	Location	Critical	
Large Laser	LA	2	5
SRM 6	CT	2	3
AMMO SRM 6 (15)	RT	1	1
CASE	RT	1	0.5
Medium Laser	LT	1	1
Medium Laser	RT	1	1
Medium Laser	RA	1	1
Medium Laser	RA	1	1
Jump Jets	RT	1	1
Jump Jets	LT	1	1
Jump Jets	LL	1	1
Jump Jets	RL	1	1

NELSON 89—

Mass: 75 tons
Chassis: FLS/HV-1
Power Plant: GM 375XL
Cruising Speed: 54 kph
Maximum Speed: 86 kph
Jump Jets: None
   Jump Capacity: None
Armor: Kemplar 5000
Armament:
   3 Selitex Radionic Large Lasers
   5 Ichiba 3000 Medium Lasers
   1 Buzzsaw Anti-Missile System
   1 Zippo Mark X Anti-Personnel Flame Gun
Manufacturer: Renault-Prime Industries
Communications System: Duoteck 195
Targeting and Tracking System: Faust/Shinji AT/TS

Overview:

The *Flashman* is one of the most underrated 'Mech designs of the Star League-era. Essentially a walking platform for a high-energy laser battery, it mounts a preponderance of energy weapons, along with the standard anti-missile cannon and an optional head-mounted antipersonnel flamer. This laser specialization makes the *Flashman* independent on the 'Mech battlefield, as it is not tied to ammunition supply lines. The *Flashman* can engage the enemy as long as its pilot remains conscious, making it one of the most sought-after designs in the Star League military.

[EDITOR'S NOTE: Fewer than 500 *Flashman* 'Mechs were operational at the beginning of the First Succession War. All were assigned to the front lines in the initial fighting. The factory complexes of the *Flashman*'s producer, Renault-Prime, were slagged in 2796, destroying all molds, prototypes, spare parts, and blueprints. The few remaining *Flashman* 'Mechs continued to operate on the front lines, until the 'Mech all but disappeared from Successor State forces. Occasionally, a *Flashman* arm, leg, or other replacement part turns up on a current design, but unless more lostech is rediscovered, there is no chance of the Inner Sphere ever seeing an intact *Flashman* again.]

Capabilities:

First produced in 2701, the FLS-8K *Flashman* is a heavy 'Mech designed for high-level combat. Its GM375XL engine is top-of-the-line engineering, generating power with unparalleled efficiency. Though not jump-capable, it is quite nimble for a 75-ton 'Mech.

The *Flashman* is one of the first designs to incorporate the new Faust/Shinji Auto-Tracking and Targeting System, which improves laser barrage fire and makes the *Flashman* one of the most accurate 'Mechs in existence.

The FLS-8K is armed with three Selitex Radionic large lasers mounted in either forearm and the center torso. Five Ichiba 3000 Medium Lasers complement their larger cousins and are mounted in the right and left torso and coaxially with the large lasers in the right and left arms. A rear-facing mount is also included, along with a Buzzsaw Anti-Missile System and a Zippo Mark X Anti-Personnel Flame Gun in a head mount beneath the pilot's cockpit. Fifteen improved SL-13 heat sinks efficiently purge the weapons of waste heat.

The *Flashman* is protected by standard Kemplar 5000 armor capable of taking extensive punishment before system failure develops.

The *Flashman* is most useful when assigned to line regiments. When more of them become available, each Assault and Heavy Lance of a regiment might include a *Flashman* to provide energy-weapon support during attacks on prepared positions or in general field combat. The 'Mech is also ideally suited for a rear-guard role when the rest of the lance runs low on ammunition. [EDITOR'S NOTE: The need to reload was the reason for many assault failures during the Succession Wars. If more 'Mechs like the *Flashman* had been available, perhaps more decisive engagements could have been conducted.]

Flashman 'Mechs usually serve as the "Fire Brigade" of an assault lance. During an advance, they follow a little to the rear, scanning for ambushes and offering supporting fire against hardpoints directed at the forward 'Mechs. In addition, when a defense force seems to waver, the *Flashman* can be utilized in a kamikaze charge, laying down fire all the way. If no reserves are available to the defenders, this tactic has a high probability of success, but when reinforcements are able to arrive, this type of action usually results in a disabled *Flashman*.

Type: **FLS-8K Flashman**

Equipment			Mass
Internal Structure:			7.5
Engine:	GM 375XL		19.25
Walking MP:	5		
Running MP:	8		
Jumping MP:	0		
Heat Sinks:	15 (30)		5
Gyro:			4
Cockpit:			3
Armor Factor:	216		13.5

	Internal Structure	Armor Value
Head	3	9
Center Torso	23	25
Center Torso (rear)		16
R/L Torso	16	22
R/L Torso (rear)		10
R/L Arm	12	24
R/L Leg	16	27

Weapons and Ammo:	Location	Critical	
Large Laser	RA	2	5
Large Laser	LA	2	5
Large Laser	CT	2	5
Medium Laser	RT	1	1
Medium Laser	LT	1	1
Medium Laser	LA	1	1
Medium Laser	RA	1	1
Medium Laser	CT(R)	1	1
Anti-Missile	RT	1	0.5
Anti-Missile Ammo (12)	RT	1	1
Flamer	H	1	1

BL6-KNT BLACK KNIGHT

Mass: 75 tons
Chassis: Technicron 1L
Power Plant: Vlar 300
Cruising Speed: 43 kph
Maximum Speed: 65 kph
Jump Jets: None
  Jump Capacity: None
Armor: Numall DuraBond Ferro-Fibrous
Armament:
  1 Magna Hellstar II PPC
  2 McCorkel Large Lasers
  4 Maxell DT Medium Lasers
  1 Magna Small Laser
Manufacturer: Kong Interstellar Corporation
Communications System: TransComm Alpha
Targeting and Tracking System: Beagle Active
  Probe

Overview:

The Star League Army introduced the *Black Knight* into service in 2578. The *Black Knight*'s heavy armor and offensive power make it the ideal command 'Mech for front-line units. At the same time, the arsenal of weapons allows the 'Mech to operate effectively on its own.

The communications system employs the latest technology to link the *Black Knight* with orbital satellites. The new Beagle Active Probe furthers the performance by picking up a much wider range of information and relaying it instantly to the pilot. The Beagle Probe can pierce standard ECM devices at short range and provide instant cataloguing of all military machines.

Capabilities:

The Black Knight supports 13 tons of Ferro-Fibrous Armor on an Endo Steel II frame. This structure provides all of the support of a standard skeleton twice its weight. The resulting lighter frame allows the 'Mech to mount a heavier weapons mix and ample armor.

If the 'Mech has a problem, it is with heat buildup. Even with 20 heat sinks, the 'Mech can still overheat quickly if the pilot is not careful with his weapon-fire selection.

The 'Mech's main weapon is the Magna Hellstar II Particle Projection Cannon, which provides quick and deadly firepower.

Twin McCorkel Large Lasers and Maxell Medium Lasers provide additional might. A head-mounted Magna small laser rounds out weaponry and offers the advantage of being tied directly to the Beagle Active Probe. This tie-in allows the Beagle's scanner to ride a low-power laser pulse through any interfering objects. Due to the limited range of the laser, this is done only for analyzing the detail of nearby objects.

Type: **BL6-KNT Black Knight**

Equipment		Mass
Internal Structure:	Endo Steel II	3.75
Engine:	Vlar 300	19
Walking MP:	4	
Running MP:	6	
Jumping MP:	0	
Heat Sinks:	20	10
Gyro:		3
Cockpit:		3
Armor Factor:	208	13

	Internal Structure	Armor Value
Head	3	9
Center Torso	23	29
Center Torso (rear)		10
R/L Torso	16	24
R/L Torso (rear)		8
R/L Arm	12	24
R/L Leg	16	24

Weapons and Ammo:	Location	Critical	
PPC	RA	3	7
Large Laser	RT	2	5
Large Laser	LT	2	5
Medium Laser	RT	1	1
Medium Laser	LT	1	1
Medium Laser	RA	1	1
Medium Laser	LA	1	1
Small Laser	H	1	0.5
Beagle Probe	CT	2	1.5

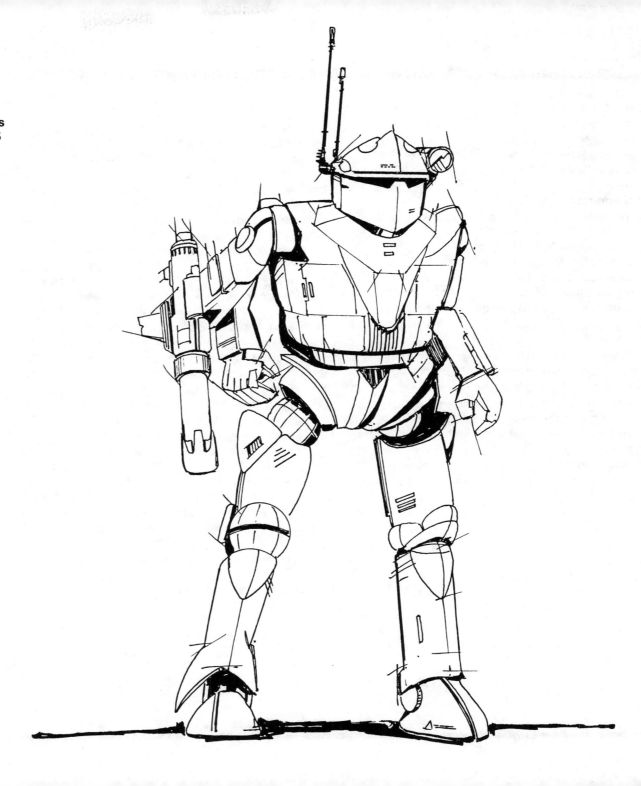

Mass: 80 tons
Chassis: Earthwerks VOL
Power Plant: Pitban 320
Cruising Speed: 43 kph
Maximum Speed: 65 kph
Jump Jets: None
    Jump Capacity: None
Armor: Mitchell Argon Ferro-Fibrous, with CASE
Armament:
    2 Tiegart Particle Cannon
    2 Bical-6 SRM Launchers
Manufacturer: Maltex Corporation
Communications System: Colmax 90
Targeting and Tracking System: TharHes Ares-5

Overview:

After years of work spent designing a competitor to the popular *Warhammer* BattleMech, the manufacturers at Maltex Corporation finally came up with the answer in 2572 with the first prototype of the *Thug*.

Building on the idea that the best defense is a strong offense, designers kept the hefty firepower of the *Warhammer*, while beefing up the armor protection and modernizing the target acquisition system. The design won great praise after initial testing and review.

Capabilities:

The *Thug*'s Ferro-Fibrous armor is its main improvement over the *Warhammer*. With the additional tonnage of armor, the *Thug* can sustain an attack for a longer time. Though carrying the same number of heat sinks as its grandfather, the *Thug* avoids some of the *Warhammer*'s problems with heat by removing secondary energy weapons and mounting double heat sinks.

The *Thug*'s main weapons are the twin Tiegart Particle Projection Cannon located in the arms. Similar to the Donal PPCs on the *Warhammer*, these cannon provide the knock-out punch needed by any heavy 'Mech. Though ten percent smaller, the Tiegart cannon matches the Donal in performance. Replacement parts are scarce, however, and fire control suffers greatly without a steady supply of parts. The system does contain several redundancy circuits, providing backup if needed.

Supporting the PPCs are two Bical-6 Short-Range Missile systems, one located in each side of the torso. These systems provide short-range firepower and free the *Thug*'s arms for hand-to-hand combat. The Short-Range Missile system and the PPCs work very well together, though rarely can all four weapons fire at the same target. When it does occur, though, such an attack is devastating, with only the strongest 'Mechs able to withstand a single barrage.

All missile loads are stored in the Cellular Ammunition Storage Equipment (CASE), which gives the *Thug* even more protection.

Type: THG-11E Thug

Equipment		Mass
Internal Structure:	Endo Steel II	4
Engine:	Pitban 320	22.5
Walking MP:	4	
Running MP:	6	
Jumping MP:	0	
Heat Sinks:	18 (36)	8
Gyro:		4
Cockpit:		3
Armor Factor:	248	15.5

	Internal Structure	Armor Value
Head	3	9
Center Torso	25	34
Center Torso (rear)		16
R/L Torso	17	25
R/L Torso (rear)		9
R/L Arm	13	26
R/L Leg	17	34

Weapons and Ammo:	Location	Critical	
PPC	RA	3	7
PPC	LA	3	7
SRM 6	RT	2	3
SRM 6	LT	2	3
AMMO SRM 6 (15)	RT	1	1
AMMO SRM 6 (15)	LT	1	1
CASE	LT	1	0.5
CASE	RT	1	0.5

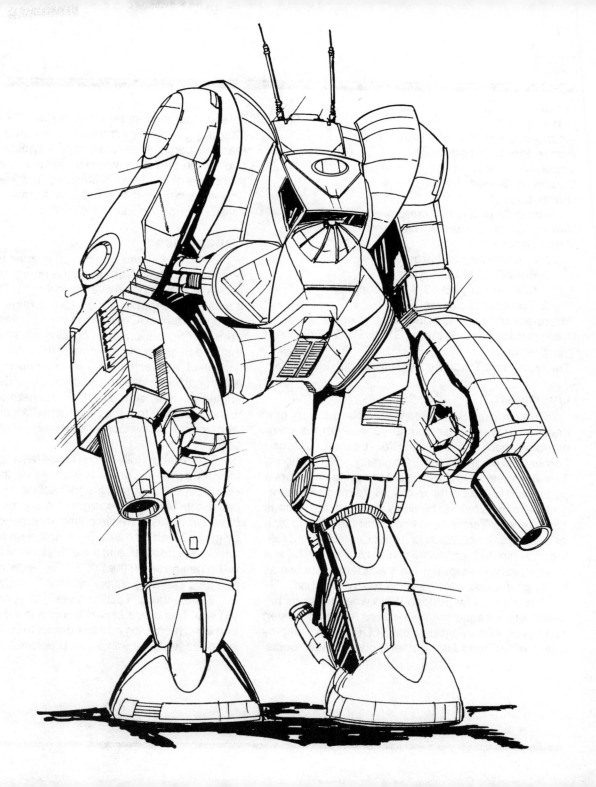

Mass: 85 tons
Chassis: Geometric 530 Hard Core
Power Plant: Strand 255D
Cruising Speed: 32 kph
Maximum Speed: 54 kph
Jump Jets: Geotec 300
   Jump Capacity: 90 meters
Armor: CarbonStrand 30 Weight AS
Armament:
   2 Blankenburg 25 Large Lasers
   2 Holly-6 SRM Launchers
   1 Blankenburg LB 10-X Autocannon
   2 Dodd Small Lasers
Manufacturer: Blankenburg Technologies
Communications System: GRPNTR Ground-
   painter 5
Targeting and Tracking System: Scope 30 RNDST

Overview:

The *Crockett* BattleMech is the classic story of a design that was better than anyone, even the commanding generals of the Star League Defense Forces, ever expected. Originally, Blankenburg Technologies of Soul won the contract to construct a battle-worthy 'Mech for use as a training simulator. The 'Mech was named for Davy Crockett, the famous 19th-Century Terran hero known for his fighting ability and unique approach to frontier combat. In 2735, the first limited production run of *Crockett*s was shipped to Star League military academies for use as training simulators for handling heavy 'Mechs.

In the era of the Hidden Wars when tensions between Star League member-states led to both overt and covert military actions, the SLDF had to redeploy many of its front-line BattleMechs to new posts, creating the need for new training 'Mechs. Ten years after the *Crockett*'s introduction, a number of commanders began to test the design for possible combat use. When they discovered its ease of handling and that some of the 'Mech's unique capabilities made it unpredictable to the enemy, a number of 'Mech divisions began to use the *Crockett*.

Capabilities:

The *Crockett* was originally designed to train new recruits and MechWarriors in the rigors, restrictions, and skills of piloting an oversized 'Mech. The fact that it was jump-capable added to the huge machine's training potential. One reason the *Crockett* made the transition from training to fighting so smoothly was that its design sacrifices some of the armor protection typical of a 'Mech of its weight class in favor of additional heat sinks and weapons. The Blankenburg engineers took seriously the Quartermaster Command's request that the new trainer-'Mech be battle-worthy and thus incorporated some powerful features.

The reliable Holly Short Range Missile Racks and their feed systems seem to work well with the *Crockett*'s Scope 30 targeting and tracking systems. Because the 'Mech was designed as a simulator, many older *Crockett*s were simplified for ease of operation by green MechWarriors. Such ergonomics made the 'Mech very popular, and these features were retained in the design when the 5003-1 Series began production as a standard heavy combat BattleMech.

Blankenburg Technologies Weapons Division (BTWD) has made breakthroughs in laser targeting and firing technology. In an attempt to give the *Crockett* an edge, Blankenburg incorporated its own specially modified laser in the 'Mech's design. The Blankenburg 25 Large Laser has a longer range than most other types because of a hyper-extensive guide beam channeled through the Scope 30 RNDST targeting system. Though the Blankenburg 25 Large Laser requires more frequent maintenance and generates more heat than other models, most warriors whose 'Mechs carry these weapons consider it a small price to pay. The light-weight, highly accurate LB 10-X Autocannon and the two arm-mounted small lasers round out the *Crockett*'s weaponry.

The cockpit life support system is the *Crockett*'s chief weakness. Because the 'Mech was conceived as a simulator rather than a fighter, its life-support apparatus and systems did not use the most durable materials. This flaw led to the deaths of three MechWarriors after the *Crockett* was pressed into full-time military service. Two years later, all 5003-1 Series 'Mechs were recalled and refitted. Meanwhile, the original design was modified to correct the flaw in new production runs of the *Crockett*.

The unique blend of movement capabilities, weapons, and their effective ranges make the *Crockett* a formidable battle machine.

[Editors Note:

The primary tactic of *Crockett* pilots was to maintain distance from an enemy, using the 'Mech's long-range lasers to slow and weaken an opponent. Then, before the enemy could accurately target the 'Mech, the pilot jumped the *Crockett* to the *rear* of the enemy. Once landed, he turned quickly to fire at an enemy BattleMech's weaker rear. If the enemy turned, he risked exposing his machine's rear to other hostile BattleMechs. This tactic was a hallmark of the *Crockett*.]

Type: **CRK 5003-1 Crockett**

Equipment		Mass
Internal Structure:		8.5
Engine:	Strand 255D	13
Walking MP:	3	
Running MP:	5	
Jumping MP:	3	
Heat Sinks:	15 (30)	5
Gyro:		3
Cockpit:		3
Armor Factor:	264	16.5

	Internal Structure	Armor Value
Head	3	9
Center Torso	27	35
Center Torso (rear)		19
R/L Torso	18	25
R/L Torso (rear)		11
R/L Arm	14	28
R/L Leg	18	36

Weapons and Ammo:	Location	Critical	
ER Large Laser	RA	2	5
ER Large Laser	LA	2	5
SRM 6	RT	2	3
SRM 6	LT	2	3
AMMO SRM 6 (30)	RT	2	2
Small Laser	RA	1	0.5
Small Laser	LA	1	0.5
LB 10-X	LT	6	11
Ammo LB 10-X(20)	RT	2	2
Ammo LB 10-X(10)	LT	1	1
Jump Jets	LL	1	1
Jump Jets	RL	1	1
Jump Jets	CT	1	1

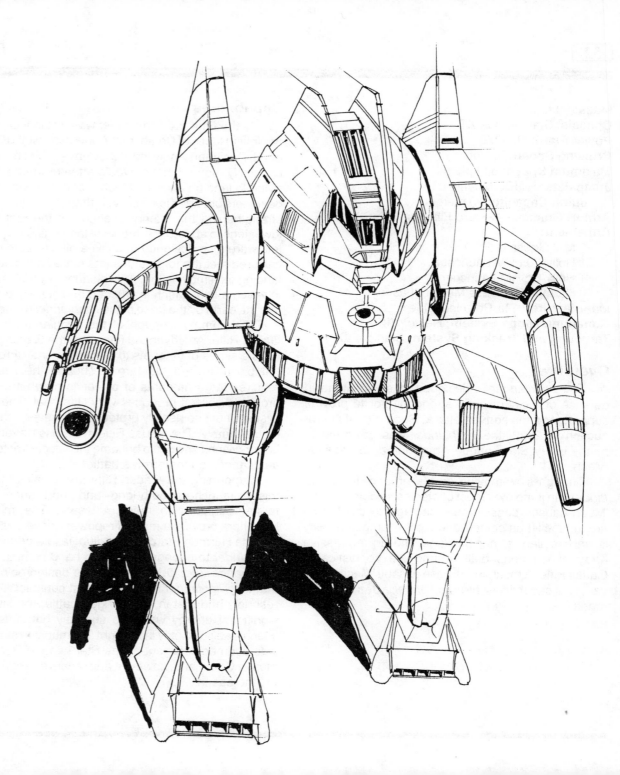

HGN-732 HIGHLANDER

Mass: 90 tons
Chassis: Star League XT
Power Plant: GM 270
Cruising Speed: 32 kph
Maximum Speed: 54 kph
Jump Jets: HildCo Model 10
  Jump Capacity: 90 meters
Armor: Grumman-3 Ferro-Fibrous, with CASE
Armament:
  1 M-7 Gauss Rifle
  1 Holly-20 LRM Launcher
  1 Holly-6 SRM Launcher
  2 Harmon Starclass Medium Lasers
Manufacturer: StarCorp Industries
Communications System: Hector VII
Targeting and Tracking System: Starlight LX-1

Overview:

The *Highlander* is designed to stand alone in defense of a city or other strongpoint or to provide support for a mixed-type attack. Soon after its introduction in 2592, the *Highlander* was assigned to nearly every Star League Army unit as an assault 'Mech.

Though slow-moving on the ground, the *Highlander* can jump over most obstacles. In doing so, the 'Mech causes considerable damage to the terrain around the lift-off point. Added to the jump capability is an excellent armor package and an impressive array of weapons built around the sophisticated Gauss Rifle. A multiple-purpose assault 'Mech with a variety of capabilities, the *Highlander* is deadly at any range.

Capabilities:

By the time the *Highlander* was introduced, the battlefield tactic of Death from Above was well-developed. Designers knew that if they gave a 'Mech jump-capability, some hotshot would attempt to use it by trying to land on another 'Mech. For that reason, the designers provided impressively thick leg armor while strengthening the interior skeleton of the feet and lower legs to absorb the impact of landings. The jump jets were also designed to allow a pilot to automatically redirect the force of his jets to compensate for landing on a moving foe. A "Highlander Burial" is one in which a light 'Mech is crushed and literally driven into the earth by the force of the *Highlander*'s landing.

The primary weapon of the *Highlander* is the Gauss Rifle. An advanced field arm, the Gauss Rifle uses a series of magnets to propel the shell through the barrel toward the target. Though the system requires large amounts of power to magnetize the projectile coils, it produces very little heat. The rifle system must be heavily protected, however, making it quite heavy. The Gauss Rifle system is perfect for larger 'Mechs and could become the successor to the autocannon on tomorrow's battlefield.

Supporting the Gauss Rifle are a pair of Holly missile launchers, both long- and short-range, and torso-mounted twin medium lasers. The missile launchers provide a mix of firepower at every range, and the Harmon Starclass medium lasers permit the *Highlander* to engage in hand-to-hand combat with both hands free. Opponents of the design point out that the *Highlander* requires almost constant ammo resupply and that in a prolonged battle, the lack of significant energy weapons severely hampers the 'Mech's ability to stay in the fight. Ammunition storage was deemed sufficient by the Star League Quartermaster Command, however, and orders for *Highlanders* increased.

The 'Mech is equipped with Grumman-3 Ferro-Fibrous Armor, and Cellular Ammunition Storage Equipment shields the shells and missiles in the right and left torso. Very reliable, the CASE system is credited with saving countless 'Mechs and pilots across the Inner Sphere.

Type: **HGN-732 Highlander**

Equipment		Mass
Internal Structure:		9
Engine:	GM 270	14.5
Walking MP:	3	
Running MP:	5	
Jumping MP:	3	
Heat Sinks:	12	2
Gyro:		3
Cockpit:		3
Armor Factor:	278	15.5

	Internal Structure	Armor Value
Head	3	9
Center Torso	29	40
Center Torso (rear)		17
R/L Torso	19	28
R/L Torso (rear)		10
R/L Arm	15	30
R/L Leg	19	38

Weapons and Ammo:	Location	Critical	
Gauss Rifle	RA	7	15
Gauss Ammo	RT	1	1
CASE	LT	1	0.5
CASE	RT	1	0.5
LRM 20	LT	5	10
AMMO LRM 20 (12)	LT	2	2
SRM 6	LA	2	3
AMMO SRM 6 (30)	LT	2	2
Medium Laser	RT	1	1
Medium Laser	RT	1	1
Jump Jets	CT	1	2
Jump Jets	LT	1	2
Jump Jets	RT	1	2

Mass: 100 tons
Chassis: Hollis Mark II
Power Plant: Vlar 300
Cruising Speed: 32 kph
Maximum Speed: 54 kph
Jump Jets: None
   Jump Capacity: None
Armor: Aldis X Ferro-Fibrous, with CASE
Armament:
   2 Deathgiver Autocannon/20s
   1 Simpson-15 LRM Launcher
   1 ExoStar Large Laser
Manufacturer: Cosara Weaponries
Communications System: Dalban Commline
Targeting and Tracking System: Dalban Hirez-B

Overview:

When General Kerensky called for the design of a powerful new 'Mech in 2741, he received blueprints for the *King Crab*, the largest 'Mech ever designed. The armor is nearly as heavy as an entire light 'Mech, with the firepower to destroy medium 'Mechs in one salvo. It is obviously not designed for speed but for sheer firepower. The Dalban electronics and communications gear are state-of-the-art, while the same Dalban Hirez-B targeting system is an engineer's showpiece, containing every piece of new technology.

[EDITOR'S NOTE: The *King Crab* entered full production but proved to be less versatile than the later 100-ton *Atlas*. Though not nearly the command vehicle the *Atlas* was, the *King Crab* was ideally suited to close fighting and remained in service. Almost all left with the Exodus.]

Capabilities:

The *King Crab* carries 16 tons of Ferro-Fibrous Armor, with no weak points in its protection. Its secondary weapons systems are the long-range missile launchers in the left torso and the large laser in the right, but its primary weapons are in its huge, handless arms. These are twin Deathgiver Autocannon/20s, among the most potent weapons ever created.

Opponents of most slow but dangerous 'Mechs try to keep their distance while attempting to pick away at the armor. The *King Crab*'s Simpson long-range missile system makes that possibility chancy at best, however. When the missiles finally run out, the *King Crab* can still blast away with its huge Exostar laser. The only proven way to destroy the 'Mech is by outnumbering it, preferably with heavy or assault 'Mechs. The *King Crab* will still wreak plenty of havoc before it goes down.

If the *King Crab* has a weakness, it is that its autocannon takes up so much space in the 'Mech's arms. Though well-armored by any standard, the arms are probably the most susceptible to damage. One internal hit to either arm will usually silence the cannon and greatly increase an enemy's chance of survival. If both cannon are lost or run out of ammo, the *King Crab* will usually retire from the field. Without constant resupply, it is little more than a large target. Though impressive, the large laser provides sufficient firepower alone to justify keeping the 'Mech in the field. Once the shelling stops, enemy 'Mechs pounce on the *King Crab* before it can make its withdrawal.

Type: **KGC-000 King Crab**

Equipment		**Mass**
Internal Structure:		10
Engine:	Vlar 300	19
Walking MP:	3	
Running MP:	5	
Jumping MP:	0	
Heat Sinks:	15	5
Gyro:		3
Cockpit:		3
Armor Factor:	287	16

	Internal Structure	Armor Value
Head	3	9
Center Torso	31	40
Center Torso (rear)		16
R/L Torso	21	30
R/L Torso (rear)		12
R/L Arm	17	34
R/L Leg	21	35

Weapons and Ammo:	**Location**	**Critical**	
AC/20	LA	10	14
AC/20	RA	10	14
AMMO AC/20 (5)	LT	1	1
AMMO AC/20 (5)	RT	1	1
CASE	LT	1	0.5
CASE	RT	1	0.5
LRM 15	LT	2	7
AMMO LRM 15 (8)	CT	1	1
Large Laser	RT	2	5

AEROSPACE FIGHTERS

Mass: 20 tons
Frame: Newhall 3P5
Engine: Rawlings 200
Armor: StarGlo Ferro-Aluminum
Armament:
   3 Omicron-Plus Medium Lasers
   1 Maxell Small Laser
Manufacturer: Newhart Industries
Communications System: 42 Transitar
Targeting and Tracking System: 0/P 3000

Overview:

Introduced in 2717, the *Trident* was designed to provide planetary defense forces with a first-response fighter featuring excellent thrust and a wide array of energy weapons.

The arrival of the *Cheetah* rendered the *Trident* obsolete. As it was rotated off frontline planetary defense, it was placed at the disposal of army commanders, where it found a new home. Its sturdy avionics and excellent speed provide commanders with the ability to outmaneuver ground-based 'Mech forces.

Capabilities:

The *Trident* was built to provide a strong punch in a small, light frame, making it ideal for carrier duty. Its 200-rated engine provides excellent power, and its frame can withstand the forces created when maneuvering at the high speeds that are the *Trident's* specialty. This frame structure is considered a paragon of design, and has influenced every fighter design since its introduction in 2717. The avionics bay features advanced motion sensors and monitoring computers to provide the pilot with a high-resolution picture of his surroundings.

The vessel mounts two tons of Ferro-Aluminum, which is similar in protective ability to the Ferro-Fibrous armor found on 'Mechs. Ferro-Aluminum is a "foamed" metal that offers equal protection with less weight and sheds heat better than conventional armor, providing the required thermal barrier during atmospheric reentry. Once equipped with standard plating, the *Trident's* armor was upgraded, primarily to provide better protection from anti-aircraft defenses.

With three medium lasers mounted to the front, the *Trident's* strafing attacks are legendary. Often, experienced pilots are able to make two or three passes on ground troops before the latter can muster a defense. The *Trident* also mounts a single rear-firing small laser. Though not effective enough to discourage an assault, the laser does provide additional protection for pilots flying without a wingman.

Type: **TRN-3T Trident**

Equipment		Mass	Weapons and Ammo:	Location	
Engine:	Rawlings 200	8.5	Medium Laser	Nose	1
Thrust	12		Medium Laser	Left Wing	1
Overthrust	18		Medium Laser	Right Wing	1
Structural Integrity:	12		Small Laser	Rear	0.5
Heat Sinks:	10	0			
Fuel:	45	3			
Cockpit:		3			
Armor Factor:	36+10	2			
	Armor Value				
Cockpit	10				
Nose	9				
Left Wing	9				
Right Wing	9				
Fuselage	5				
Engine	4				

SWF-606 SWIFT

Mass: 25 tons
Frame: Mujika-L9 Aerospace
Engine: Shinobi 275-A
Armor: KX4 Ferro-Aluminum
Armament:
    1 Maxell-UD6 Medium Laser
    1 McCorkel Small Laser
Manufacturer: Caletra Fighters
Communications System: Lockheed Matrix-V
Targeting and Tracking System: PhantomTrac 55

Overview:

Originally scheduled for unveiling in 2675, the *Swift* was repeatedly delayed. Avionic problems, regulator difficulties, and "gremlins" were all blamed for the late deployment, but when the *Swift* was finally released, commanders and pilots discovered the real reasons for the long wait. The *Swift's* 25 tons are packed with every aeronautic feature available. Computers monitor every aspect of the ship's flight, speaking directly to the pilot via voice synthesizer. Many of the pilot's most complex functions are performed by the computer systems instead. The most maneuverable aerospace craft yet designed, the *Swift* can dance circles around any fighter in the Inner Sphere, and is equally at home in zero-G or heavy gravity.

Capabilities:

Because of its small size and low-fuel capacity, the *Swift* is based on carriers to provide quick response for protecting jump points. On its first mission in 2682, however, a *Swift* crashed into the carrier *Oliver Jones* while attempting to dock. The pilot and the flight-control deck reported a normal flight approach when the *Swift's* primary systems monitor suddenly reported critical damage to the fuselage. Without further warning, the pilot was ejected from the craft. The *Swift* continued its flight path, crashing into the flight deck. There were no deaths, but damage was extensive. The craft's flight recorder and memory core were destroyed when the crash set off 20 tons of fighter fuel on the flight deck. The SLDF pulled all the new *Swifts* out of service while investigators tried to figure out what had gone wrong. Six months of tests revealed little, and the *Swift* re-entered service, with the cause of the accident listed only as "electronic failure."

The master computer, the B-TT7i (known affectionately by pilots as Betty or Bouncing Betty), provides pilots with critical information more quickly than earlier models. Though Betty works perfectly, pilots say her "friendly warnings" sound like nagging. Many pilots disengage the B-TT7i once the craft is airborne.

For all its advanced avionics, the *Swift* carries only a single Maxell UD6 medium laser and a single McCorkel small laser, both mounted in the nose. These weapons give the *Swift* the ability to sting an enemy, but little more. Though lightly armed, the *Swift* has good acceleration and its Ferro-Aluminum armor can absorb considerable punishment, allowing it to engage opponents with superior weaponry. The SLDF has redeployed some *Swifts* to ground bases. Some commanders believe that the *Swift's* use of energy weapons makes it an ideal air-to-ground attack craft.

Type: **SWF-606 Swift**

Equipment		Mass		Weapons and Ammo:	Location	
Engine:	Shinobi 275-A	15.5		Medium Laser	Nose	1
Thrust	13			Small Laser	Nose	0.5
Overthrust	21					
Structural Integrity:	13					
Heat Sinks:	10	0				
Fuel:	45	3				
Cockpit:		3				
Armor Factor:	36+10	2				

	Armor Value
Cockpit	10
Nose	10
Left Wing	8
Right Wing	8
Fuselage	6
Engine	4

Mass: 30 tons
Frame: F-50/C
Engine: GM 150
Armor: Carbondale III
Armament:
    1 Starcutter Particle Projection Cannon
    1 Allied Technologies Model 2 Medium Laser
    1 Allied Technologies Model 1 Small Laser
Manufacturer: New Age Systems Inc.
Communications System: CMDSTAT 400-D
Targeting and Tracking System: Scope Paint

Overview:

The SPD-502 *Spad* is considered one of the best fighters in the Star League Defense Forces. One of the outstanding features of this space fighter is its durability. Designed with simple repairs in mind, every part of the *Spad* is easy to access, remove, and replace. Furthermore, all components were designed for modular access, so that if one system type should fail, any number of similar systems from different manufacturers could replace it. The net result is a fighter ready to go virtually anywhere at any time.

Capabilities:

The *Spad* carries no weapons that require reloading, which means that it is not restricted by ammunition and weight factors. The primary weapon is the Starcutter PPC mounted in the nose of the craft.

The secondary weapons are the Allied Technologies small and medium lasers. The medium laser is mounted further back on the fuselage in front of the cockpit. This laser resembles the old-fashioned, mounted machine gun on bi-plane fighters of 20th Century Terra.

The Allied Model 1 small laser is mounted directly behind the cockpit and is fully rotational, allowing the *Spad* to fire to the rear at pursuing ships. A protective cowling folds over the laser during atmospheric re-entry to protect its systems and give the fighter a more aerodynamic profile. The weapon has to be covered only for the few minutes of re-entry burn before being redeployed in the atmosphere.

The *Spad*'s sloped-wing design and special alloy wing-tips help make it project electonic "echoes" that wreak havoc on many enemy targeting systems. The *Spad* is often confused with a larger AeroSpace Fighter.

For armor, the *Spad* has the highly praised Carbondale III plating system. This system uses individual plates of armor woven in a manner to deflect laser shots once they penetrate the outer skin.

The GM 150 engine is a proven unit that holds up well in-flight and on the ground. Safely insulated with Carbondale III armor, the GM 150 can carry a pilot through heavy fire with a good deal of confidence. On the ground, the GM 150 can be detached and removed in a matter of six hours, compared to the average 10.35 hours for engine replacement in other Star League fighter craft.

Type: **SPD-502 Spad**

Equipment		Mass
Engine:	GM 150	5.5
Thrust	7	
Overthrust	11	
Structural Integrity:	7	
Heat Sinks:	10	0
Fuel:	75	5
Cockpit:		3
Armor Factor:	128+10	8

	Armor Value
Cockpit	25
Nose	25
Left Wing	18
Right Wing	18
Fuselage	27
Engine	25

Weapons and Ammo:	Location	
PPC	Nose	7
Medium Laser	Fuselage	1
Small Laser	Fuselage	0.5

Mass: 35 tons
Frame: Saroyan Cavalier
Engine: Bangkock 140
Armor: SlabPanzer V
Armament:
    1 Holly-10 Long Range Missile Launcher
    1 BLW Blow Mark III Large Laser
    1 BLW Blow Mark II Medium Laser
Manufacturer: Blow/Hookson
Communications System: Orbitcom Model 11
Targeting and Tracking System: PS/1/12

Overview:

When Blow/Hookson Technologies took on the challenge of designing the AeroSpace Fighter that would eventually be known as the *Zero*, or ZRO-114, it might have seemed an impossible task. Their assignment was to create a light fighter with heavy firepower in a variety of range classes, that was also fast and better-armored than most light fighters.

The Blow/Hookson engineers gave the *Zero* a bold, fresh appearance, with narrow, rounded wings, thinly profiled and mounted directly in front of the cockpit. This protects the pilot from ground-fire shrapnel that could shatter the delicate cockpit systems during ground assaults. The engine cooling system is also in front of the cockpit, further protecting the pilot.

The specification for this light fighter called for a weapons complement that operated over a variety of ranges. To accomplish this, the *Zero* mounts the reliable Holly long-range missile delivery racks as well as two dependable laser systems. The *Zero* made a strong impression when it first appeared in 2703. It has since become one of the most respected and honored of the light fighters assigned to the outer edges of the vast Inner Sphere.

Capabilities:

Many small fighters of the *Zero*'s weight class tend to mount a variety of weapons, while the *Zero* concentrates on only two: lasers and missiles. The widely used Holly LRM system is popular, while the large and small lasers are both of Blow/Hookson manufacture. The Blow Mark III large laser uses five concentrations of firepower, ranging from a wide beam that does not inflict much damage but does disrupt the target's electronics and tracking systems, to a concentrated beam that can sear through even the most advanced armor. The pilot can control these settings, in contrast to other lasers that must be adjusted prior to combat by a ground-crew technician. The Blow Mark II medium laser system does not offer the same flexibility, however, and is always set for a concentrated beam. Both systems are dependable and durable even during the most adverse combat situations.

The *Zero*'s narrow wings resemble those of the original *Zero* fighter from the Second World War-era on Terra. Those on the 2RO-1121 are retractable, folding to the rear of the craft. In atmosphere, this gives the *Zero* such a fast rate of dive that it can catch even experienced fighters off-guard. Further, the pilot can begin a landing, then extend the fighter's wings to angle the craft properly, which gives it the ability to bounce off the atmosphere from a lower altitude in a controlled manner. This is a favorite tactic of *Zero* pilots when near an atmosphere.

The fighter's only known drawback is that the fuel system is dispersed throughout the craft, using five different fuel tanks. Fuel lines inter-linking the different tanks run the length of the fighter to provide fuel to the engines. If the battle computer is damaged or one of the lines is severed, five tons of fuel can become only a ton's worth in a matter of seconds. The fuel lines are heavily shielded, but *Zero* pilots must still be aware of the potential proble.

[Editor's Note: When a group of unknown DropShips began to bomb the cities of Kujan Minor and Hickston on New Roland near the Periphery, the Star League Defense Forces were quick to respond by sending in the Third RCT of the 89th BattleMech Division under General Gaffa Pardoe. With him was the new fighter, the first production run of *Zero*s ever created.

Upon arrival at the system nadir jump point, the General encountered a group of ships outnumbering him almost two to one. From his command ship, the General ordered his aerospace forces to fly in the opposite direction of the enemy, away from the range of their sensors. Then, in a bold move, he sent the rest of his unit charging headlong into the midst of the unknown enemy.

Without fighter protection, the Third RCT took a pounding, but Pardoe held on. Meanwhile, his fighters, led by a squadron of the new *Zero*s, skirted around the battle to reach the enemy's rear. Moving at incredible speeds and seemingly out of nowhere, the *Zero*s dove in on the task force. Backed up with a flight of *Chippewa* heavy fighters, they destroyed the enemy flagship within the first four minutes of engagement. The other vessels broke and staggered into what remained of Pardoe's task force. Within an hour, the Third had destroyed the enemy's main ships, leaving only their ground forces stranded on New Roland.

Wasting no time, the General ordered his fighters to refuel and to head to the planet. In the two days' fighting, the *Zero*s proved themselves. Taking only minimal losses, they managed to destroy greatly superior numbers. In the end, Pardoe discovered that his opponent was a crack undercover unit from the Rim Worlds Republic, and that it had been raiding the Davion and Liao border regions for several months. Though the Rim Worlds disclaimed any knowledge of the "renegades," Pardoe received the highest commendations for his fast and furious actions.]

Type: **ZRO-114 Zero**

Equipment		Mass
Engine:	Bangkock140	5
Thrust	6	
Overthrust	9	
Structural Integrity:	6	
Heat Sinks:	10	0
Fuel:	75	5
Cockpit:		3
Armor Factor:	160+10	10

	Armor Value
Cockpit	25
Nose	40
Left Wing	20
Right Wing	20
Fuselage	30
Engine	35

Weapons and Ammo:	Location	
LRM10	Nose	5
AMMO LRM 10 (12)	Fuselage	1
Large Laser	Nose	5
Medium Laser	Fuselage	1

Mass: 40 tons
Frame: Shipil 10R
Engine: GM 200
Armor: StarGlo Ferro-Aluminum
Armament:
     2 Starflash-1A Medium Lasers
     2 Holly-8 LRM Delivery Systems
Manufacturer: Iona Light Shipyards
Communications System: Rander 300
Targeting and Tracking System: SynCom Master

Overview:

   A medium-weight fighter designed primarily for zero-G flight, the *Rogue* provides commanders with a flying missile platform. Poorly equipped for a dogfight, the *Rogue* needs the company of other fighters.

   Though the *Rogue* is not as nimble as some pilots might like, none would complain about its armor. Upon returning to base, *Rogue* pilots are often astonished to see how much punishment their ship has sustained.

Capabilities:

   Sluggish at the controls, the *Rogue* must rely on armor and firepower to carry the day. The *Rogue* carries five tons of fuel, giving it the ability to conduct patrols and participate in guard duty. When an attack is expected, *Rogue*s usually launch first to provide cover for other craft. The *Rogue* also carries five and one-half tons of the most advanced armor in the Star League.

   The *Rogue*'s primary weapons systems are its wing-mounted, Holly-8 LRM-15 launchers. Though heavy and bulky, the LRMs make the *Rogue* a threat at extreme distances. The *Rogue* carries only eight reloads for each system, however, leaving it ill-equipped to fight prolonged engagements. The *Rogue* is usually the first fighter into the fray, but it is also the first one to leave.

   Two Starflash medium lasers back up the LRMs. The front-mounted laser is useful in a dogfight, but the fighter is more likely to use the rear-mounted laser to discourage pursuit.

[Editor's Note: The RGU-133F model packs short-range missiles instead of the LRM launchers. Each wing carries two SRM-5 racks and two tons of missiles, providing 30 reloads on each side. Class F Rogues are usually ground-based fighters, fitted to carry bombs.

   The RGU-133L exchanges the LRM launchers and their ammunition for two large lasers and six additional heat sinks. Class L has proved effective in strafing attacks.]

Type: **RGU-133E Rogue**

Equipment		Mass
Engine:	GM 200	8.5
Thrust	7	
Overthrust	11	
Structural Integrity:	7	
Heat Sinks:	10	0
Fuel:	75	5
Cockpit:		3
Armor Factor:	99+10	5.5

	Armor Value
Cockpit	15
Nose	20
Left Wing	22
Right Wing	22
Fuselage	20
Engine	10

Weapons and Ammo:	Location	
Medium Laser	Nose	1
LRM 15	Right Wing	7
AMMO LRM 15 (8)	Right Wing	1
LRM 15	Left Wing	7
AMMO LRM 15 (8)	Left Wing	1
Medium Laser	Rear	1

THK-63 TOMAHAWK

Mass: 45 tons
Frame: Shipil 35-B
Engine: PlasmaStar 270
Armor: Fiber 10 Ferro-Aluminum
Armament:
  1 ExoStar IV Small Laser
  2 Maxell SR Large Lasers
Manufacturer: Wanker Aerospace
Communications System: Telestar Fortran
Targeting and Tracking System: IMB 5000

Overview:

The *Tomahawk*'s forte is dogfighting, either in space or in a planetary atmosphere. It can outmaneuver heavy craft and outshoot light fighters. The *Tomahawk*'s most effective use is flying close-escort for fighters with long-range weapons.

The *Tomahawk* is something of a hothead, however. Despite the addition of two heat sinks, the craft fairly shimmers when in combat. Initial testing on prototypes in 2642 showed abnormally high heat signatures, and so designers installed the two extra heat sinks, along with Ferro-Aluminum armor, mitigating the problem somewhat.

Capabilities:

The *Tomahawk* mounts ten tons of Ferro-Aluminum armor, much more protection than any other craft of its class.

The two large lasers on the wings provide excellent air-to-ground capabilities. In a dogfight, the lasers provide good firepower but quickly start to overheat the *Tomahawk*. By 2880, the *Tomahawk* was disdained by pilots because of the heat problem. Engineers decided the *Tomahawk* was a prime candidate for testing double heat sinks in an AeroSpace Fighter. The modified *Tomahawk* excelled in tests and in the field, and so the thousands of *Tomahawk*s have been retrofitted with double heat sinks, despite the great expense.

Designers mounted the small laser in the nose more out of tradition than utility. Though the small laser is of little use, designers feared that pilots would balk at a fighter without a weapon in its nose.

[Editor's Note: The only variant of the *Tomahawk* is the THK-53, which was an earlier attempt to resolve the heat problem. Each wing holds three medium lasers and two additional heat sinks. A half-ton of armor replaces the small laser in the nose. The change was insufficient to solve the overheating problems, and so few fighters of this design exist.]

Type: **THK-63 Tomahawk**

Equipment			Mass
Engine:	PlasmaStar 270		14.5
Thrust	8		
Overthrust	12		
Structural Integrity:	8		
Heat Sinks:	12(24)		2
Fuel:	75		5
Cockpit:			3
Armor Factor:	179+10		10
		Armor Value	
Cockpit		15	
Nose		40	
Left Wing		30	
Right Wing		30	
Fuselage		49	
Engine		25	

Weapons and Ammo:	Location	
Small Laser	Nose	0.5
Large Laser	Right Wing	5
Large Laser	Left Wing	5

Mass: 50 tons
Frame: Wakazashi IX
Engine: Rawlings 250
Armor: SRT Ferro-Aluminum
Armament:
    2 Diverse Optics/A Large Lasers
    1 Starflash Medium Laser
Manufacturer: Mitchell Vehicles
Communications System: Telecron L50
Targeting and Tracking System: Beagle Active
    Probe

Overview:

Commissioned in 2710, the *Hellcat II* is one of the newest fighters of the Star League Defense Forces. This makes it one of the least known aircraft flying, and its simple design makes it one of the least recognizable. The *Hellcat*'s primary duty is to carry the Beagle Active Probe into aerospace combat, though it can also hold its own with other aircraft in its weight class.

The *Hellcat* excels as a heavy aerospace scout. With good speed and excellent avionics, it can avoid nearly any fight not of the pilot's own choosing, and with the recent addition of the most powerful scanning device in the Star League, the chances of anyone ambushing a *Hellcat* are small.

Capabilities:

The *Hellcat*'s test pilots called it a flying tank because the weight of its standard armor was excessive. Three tons of armor were removed to improve its handling characteristics, but commanders felt that the aircraft's increased vulnerability reduced its chances of completing its primary mission. Designers solved both problems by switching to Ferro-Aluminum armor, which provides significantly greater protection than standard armor of the same weight. It also provides excellent heat dissipation, making it a natural for AeroSpace Fighters. Though Ferro-Aluminum is more expensive than standard armor, field commanders persuaded procurement officers to pay whatever necessary for the superior product.

Two wing-mounted Diverse Optics large lasers are linked directly to the Beagle Active Probe, which makes the lasers extremely accurate at any range. Though bulky, these primary weapons provide the *Hellcat* with sufficient firepower for frontal attack. Its only other weapon is a rear-firing medium laser placed to help the *Hellcat* in retreat. Pilots joke that in a *Hellcat* they are better at shooting over their shoulders than straight ahead.

The Beagle Active Probe is the latest in detection equipment. It has the longest range of any scanner available and is able to pierce standard jamming devices at a much longer range than any other. Built into the Beagle is a state-of-the-art memory system, which provides the pilot with information on previous damage, abilities, and fighting style of any 'Mech, fighter, or ground vehicle it has ever encountered. It can even forecast probable enemy moves, based on previous experience. The Beagle has also received high marks as a training device, as it can recreate any situation on its tactical display. Pilots use a joystick to enter in alternate actions and then are able to see the consequences of tactical changes. This new system is among the most requested pieces of hardware in the SLDF.

Type: **HCT-213B Hellcat II**

Equipment		Mass
Engine:	Rawlings 250	12.5
Thrust	7	
Overthrust	11	
Structural Integrity:	7	
Heat Sinks:	15	5
Fuel:	75	5
Cockpit:		3
Armor Factor:	215+10	12

	Armor Value
Cockpit	15
Nose	50
Left Wing	38
Right Wing	38
Fuselage	52
Engine	32

Weapons and Ammo:	Location	
Medium Laser	Rear	1
Large Laser	Right Wing	5
Large Laser	Left Wing	5
Beagle Active Probe	Nose	1.5

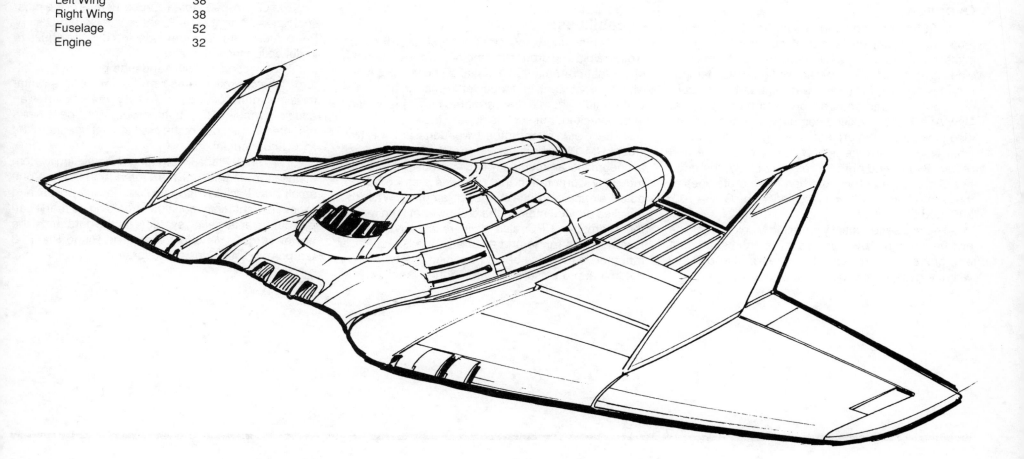

Mass: 60 tons
Frame: Saroyan 2.5
Engine: Piker 180
Armor: Carbondale IV Ferro-Aluminum
Armament:
2 Holly-15 Long Range Missile Launchers
1 Starcutter Particle Projection Cannon
4 Allied Technologies Model 2 Medium Lasers
2 Allied Technologies Model 1 Small Lasers
Manufacturer: New Age Systems Inc.
Communications System: COMSTAT 500 ATM
Targeting and Tracking System: Ringo Plant 88

Overview:

In 2654, the engineering staff at New Age Systems Inc. sought out some of the greatest fighter pilots in the Star League Defense Forces to assist in a design project for a new medium fighter. On temporary assignment for three years, these five officers offered their ideas and opinions to the designers at New Age. Several skilled combat-repair technicians also took part in the project, offering suggestions on what would make the fighter easier to service and repair. By the end of the three-year study, the engineers at New Age Systems had three prototypes of the same class of fighter, classified as the GTHA 100, 300, and 500 Gotha.

The 100 series initially patrolled Marik space. The engine, though providing less thrust than some others, proved very reliable. Pilots were also pleased with the number and variety of weapons.

The 300 Series reduced the weapons in favor of heavier armor protection. This model has 16 tons of armor, far more than most medium fighters. This series was less well received than the 100 series, mostly because the bulky armor makes the craft difficult to handle in an atmosphere.

The GTHA-500 Gotha is the best of the three. It carries a variety of weapons, both long- and short-range. The 500 carries 13 tons of armor, thanks to the pilots who assisted in its design. Such a balance has proven itself useful in a variety of tasks for almost a century, and the GTHA-500 is expected to be a mainstay of the SLDF for many years to come.

Capabilities:

The medium-weight class of AeroSpace Fighters is often a playing ground for engineers and designers. Many fast craft exist in this class, including several with a great deal of firepower. Among these, the Gotha might seem a slow, armored target just waiting to be attacked, but such is not the case.

The Gotha's long-range weapons are the twin Holly LRM-15 racks in the wings of the craft. They use a pneumatic ammunition-feed system patented by the Holly Corporation that provides a smooth feed, quick reloads, and little chance of jamming. While the missiles provide most of the firepower at long range, the Starcutter PPC also delivers massive punch. Known for its range and accuracy, the Starcutter is mounted in the nose behind a sliding safety/re-entry hatch that protects the weapon during landing.

The supporting firepower for close range is a combination of four medium and two small lasers, all manufactured by New Age Systems' wholly-owned subsidiary, Allied Technologies. These models have proven reliable, and their standard, coil-cooling insulation has been modified to weld tightly with the Gotha's armor.

The weapon placements on the Gotha show the pilots' influence during the design. The two rear-mounted Allied medium lasers have full interface with the Ringo Plant 88 targeting and tracking system. These weapons make it dangerous for a light enemy fighter to maneuver itself onto the Gotha's tail.

The GTHA-500 Gotha carries 13 tons of the most sophisticated armor ever created, the CarbonDale IV Ferro-Aluminum. The sleek design is quite effective in deflecting incoming shots.

The ejection system sends the pilot out the bottom of the cockpit to keep him clear of the long-range missile exhaust or scopes. The Gotha also carries an additional four CBT Chamberpot Class heat sinks mounted in the nose of the craft to vent heat from the PPC and medium lasers.

The Ringo Plant 88 targeting and tracking system installed in all three of the Gotha models, has one small drawback. When initialized at full power and range, it creates so much electronic noise that it can jam out other targeting systems for the duration of the power surge. This effect blinds the Ringo Plant 88 temporarily, but it does recalibrate quickly.

Type: **GTHA-500 Gotha**

Equipment		Mass
Engine:	Piker 180	7
Thrust	5	
Overthrust	7	
Structural Integrity:	6	
Heat Sinks:	14	4
Fuel:	90	6
Cockpit:		3
Armor Factor:	233+10	13

	Armor Value
Cockpit	20
Nose	60
Left Wing	46
Right Wing	46
Fuselage	31
Engine	40

Weapons and Ammo:	Location	
PPC	Nose	7
LRM 15	Right Wing	7
LRM 15	Left Wing	7
AMMO LRM 15 (8)	Fuselage	1
Medium Laser	Nose	1
Medium Laser	Nose	1
Medium Laser	Rear	1
Medium Laser	Rear	1
Small Laser	Right Wing	0.5
Small Laser	Left Wing	0.5

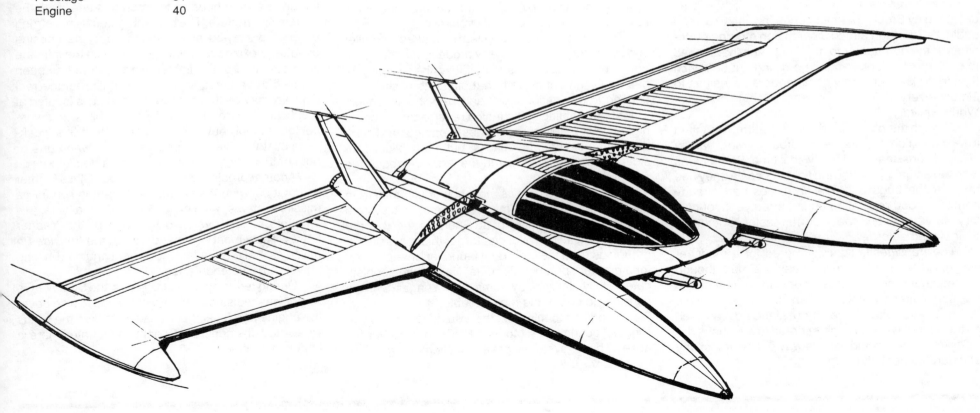

Mass: 65 tons
Frame: Lockheed FairFax
Engine: Thankor 260
Armor: SearWeave
Armament:
    5 Yeager-6 Short Range Missile Delivery
        Systems
    2 Ringer Technologies Model 1 Particle
        Projection Cannon
    2 Allied Technologies Model 2 Medium Lasers
Manufacturer: Brooks Manufacturing Inc.
Communications System: OP/1/2/3.66
Targeting and Tracking System: Ryder Track II

Overview:

The *Ironsides* Class AeroSpace Fighter was designed by Brooks Manufacturing Inc. in 2613, then publicized through a media campaign offering prototypes of the new fighter to any SLDF unit that wished to evaluate it. Brooks ended up giving out 500 such fighters to Regular Army commanders as well as to almost every House Army and even to the Rim Worlds military.

Though this ploy was costly for the firm, it resulted in their new fighter being field-tested in a wider variety of conditions than usual. By the time Brooks was ready to actually produce the fighter for sale, they had most of the bugs out. The *Ironsides* had already earned a good reputation during three years of military service before the Quartermaster Command ever placed an order.

The *Ironsides* is lightly armored for a medium-weight fighter. It is, however, heavily armed, though inadequately cooled. It is fearsome in combat due to the sheer firepower that it can deliver in a single volley. Even pilots of larger, more standard craft such as the *Chippewa* heavy fighter dread to encounter the *Ironsides*, which could fight its way out of almost any standard combat situation.

Capabilities:

The *Ironsides* Class Fighter fills many gaps in current fighter technology because it is armed with a wide range of weaponry that can also target all its systems effectively. The core of this system is the Ryder Track II targeting and tracking system. Using a series of sensors placed throughout the craft, it tracks simultaneously from several locations rather from a single, central one. This provides for better targeting. Also, the Ryder system can be programmed for a variety of different weapon types without the need for time-consuming or space-eating accessories. Thus, the *Ironsides* pilot is able to fire a simultaneous volley of short-range missiles, PPCs, and lasers, accurately controlling the fire on all weapons. The success of this system is borne out by the fact that several other firms have copied the unpatented circuitry.

The IRN-SD1 engine system is markedly smaller and more compact than many models with the same power output ratio. This is because the fusion core has an alignment system that alters its position according to gravitational pull and velocity influences. This subtle shifting of the fusion reactor core allows a higher power-yield curve with less space. The system does have several drawbacks, but many pilots consider the tradeoff well worth the extra weapons the *Ironsides* can carry.

The *Ironsides* gets its most powerful punch from the Yeager short-range missile system. This system is able to launch a volley of 30 Short-Range Ramrod Class missiles. The pilot can target these missiles in groupings from the individual launcher or separately for a greater spread of damage. Next to the sophisticated Holly delivery systems, the Yeager SRM is considered one of the most reliable.

In addition to missiles, the *Ironsides* mounts two Ringer Technologies Model 1 PPCs in its rather flat nose. These systems have excellent range. The Ryder targeting and tracking system allows the PPCs to fire after a volley of SRMs have been launched without disrupting the missiles' flight path or inadvertently hitting any of the volley. This will very quickly overheat the fighter, however. The Ringer Model 1s both use a high-density chamber coil that provides for a tighter stream of charged-particle energy. This beam is narrower than that of many other PPCs but packs the same punch. The net result is more concentrated hitting power against a smaller area.

The *Ironsides* also carries two Allied Technologies Model 2 medium lasers, the only weak link in the fighter's weapons systems. This weapon has an energy housing problem that has not been resolved after many years. If the lasers are fired extensively, the power-chain housing that controls energy to the system can rupture. The coolant system is not strong enough to support any breakage and the housing eventually explodes, causing damage in the intricate wing structure of the fighter. This system has been recalled three times for improvements, but the real difficulty may be that the power housing is located at a critical juncture of the wing assemblies. It is suspected, though never been proven, that this weakness cost the lives of three aeropilots when one or both of their wings exploded during a dogfight.

Another problem with the *Ironsides* Class Fighter is that it does not carry sufficient ammunition for its missile systems. With only 15 reloads available, this amounts to just over two for each of the Yeager SRMs. Thus, most commanders use the *Ironsides* in missions that require fast movement and hard-hitting power, but little endurance.

During redesign of the *Ironsides*, the SearWeave Armor was redistributed from the wings to also cover the engine and fuselage. Because this left the wings weakened, the number of weapons mounted there is kept to a minimum.

Type: **IRN-SD1 Ironsides**

Equipment		Mass
Engine:	Thankor 260	13.5
Thrust	6	
Overthrust	9	
Structural Integrity:	7	
Heat Sinks:	10(20)	0
Fuel:	75	5
Cockpit:		3
Armor Factor:	176+10	11

	Armor Value
Cockpit	15
Nose	40
Left Wing	25
Right Wing	25
Fuselage	41
Engine	40

Weapons and Ammo:	Location	
SRM 6	Nose	3
SRM 6	Right Wing	3
SRM 6	Right Wing	3
SRM 6	Left Wing	3
SRM 6	Left Wing	3
AMMO SRM 6 (15)	Fuselage	1
PPC	Nose	7
PPC	Nose	7
Medium Laser	Right Wing	1
Medium Laser	Left Wing	1

Mass: 75 tons
Frame: Lockheed BR65
Engine: Pitban C375
Armor: Boeing C-tran Ferro-Aluminum
Armament:
    1 Imperator Zeta-20 Autocannon
Manufacturer: Boeing Interstellar
Communications System: Lassitor FibroLink
Targeting and Tracking System: BANDAR 9

Overview:

The *Hammerhead* is an older design that still poses a threat to more modern craft. With its powerful Zeta 20 autocannon, the *Hammerhead* can end a battle quickly. *Hammerhead*s are most often deployed in defensive roles, protecting planets or patrolling jump points. The *Hammerhead* has excellent acceleration for a fighter of its size.

Capabilities:

Normally based on the ground, *Hammerhead*s require too much room and supplies to use a carrier. The *Hammerhead* carries an operational load of five tons of fuel to feed the large engine, which gives it acceptable flight speeds.

Engineers added the Ferro-Aluminum armor more than a century after the *Hammerhead* entered service in 2407. Like many retrofits, the armor is ungainly in some areas and weak in others. Despite these problems, the additional protection has added years to the *Hammerhead*'s service. Significantly stronger than standard armor plating of the same weight, Ferro-Aluminum gives better protection than slab armor. In addition, Ferro-Aluminum sheds heat quickly, providing critical protection during atmospheric re-entry.

The single weapon system of the *Hammerhead* is the huge autocannon, which skeptics considered impractical for use in space. The *Hammerhead*'s initial contacts were with light or medium fighters, allowing it to rack up an impressive string of kills before the first one was lost during fighting in the Periphery.

Because it lacks supporting weapons, the *Hammerhead* cannot remain in combat for long periods. The craft carries three tons of large shells for its autocannon, but a prolonged battle can leave the *Hammerhead* weaponless. For this reason, most commanders team *Hammerhead*s with fighters that use energy weapons.

Type: **HMR-HD Hammerhead**

Equipment		Mass
Engine:	Pitban C375	38.5
Thrust	7	
Overthrust	11	
Structural Integrity:	8	
Heat Sinks:	10	0
Fuel:	75	5
Cockpit:		3
Armor Factor:	206+10	11.5

	Armor Value
Cockpit	16
Nose	60
Left Wing	40
Right Wing	40
Fuselage	40
Engine	20

Weapons and Ammo:	Location	
AC/20	Nose	14
AMMO AC/20 (15)	Nose	3

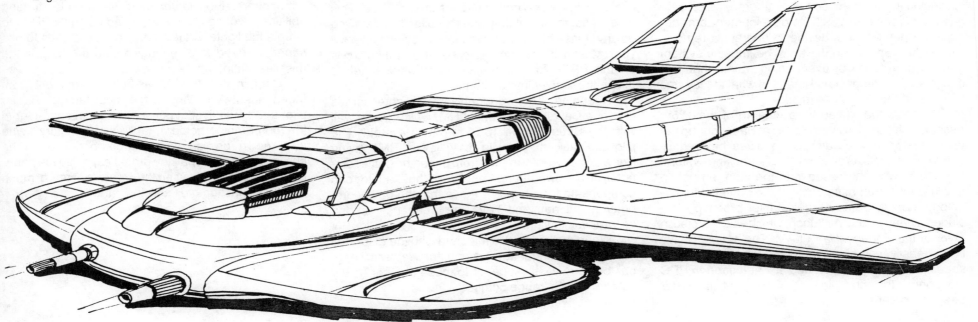

Mass: 85 tons
Frame: Interstar 290M
Engine: AeroFord 340
Armor: PhilterMesh
Armament:
   1 RNG Ranger Autocannon
   2 PDVR Piledriver Model 11-D Particle Projection
    Cannon
   1 Cavalier Industries LRM-10 System
Manufacturer: Bauer Enterprises
Communications System: COMHRT II.Q
Targeting and Tracking System: Scope 130Y

Overview:

When Bauer Enterprises of Tharkad, a manufacturer of children's electronic toys, decided to begin producing heavy AeroSpace Fighters, it was definitely a surprise. In 2590, its development arm designed a neurocontrol device to operate a remote-piloted AeroSpace Fighter toy. The impulse system generated a series of overlapping waves that produced a three-dimensional image of what the toy was "seeing" in the operator's mind.

Doctor Lionel Rajan III, a veteran of the 125th Assault Company, was employed at Bauer during the toy's development. It was his idea to use the overlapping wave signals as an element of a tracking system. The SLDF was impressed with the idea, and soon after Bauer Enterprises entered the battlefield technology market. Some of their earlier prototypes included a heavy Land-Air 'Mech, which was rejected in favor of the *Phoenix Hawk* LAM. The *Rapier* heavy fighter easily won approval, however. With its high-speed turning capability and its autocannon/PPC weaponry, the craft looked worthy of the Star League's arsenals.

Within four years, a Tharkad factory was producing *Rapier*s full-time. Despite some initial difficulties, the fighter eventually proved successful, filling the weight slot just below the *Chippewa*, the heaviest of the Star League's fighter forces.

Capabilities:

The *Rapier* can create havoc with its nose-mounted, Ranger class autocannon, whose Bauer-Scope 130Y tracking system gives it a range beyond most weapons of the type. Twin PDVR Piledriver Model 11-D PPCs give the fighter its shorter-range punch. These are mounted on opposite sides of the cockpit, which caused some difficulties in the fighter's early career. The developmental models of the *Rapier* tended to shut down the heating/cooling system in the cockpit when both weapons fired at once. This defect cost the life of only one test pilot, but it slowed down release of the improved model by almost a full year. Most pilots still double-check the venting cowls on the PPCs for the proper modifications before taking the *Rapier* into combat.

Rounding off the weaponry that the fighter carries is a lone Cavalier Industries LRM, which works well with the Bauer-Scope 130Y targeting system. The pilot can track each missile of a volley of LRMs, giving it new targeting information from either the battlecomputer or his own neural impulses. Thus, a pilot can compensate for an enemy move that the battlecomputer might not, and have the weapons respond accordingly in flight.

When the LRM-10 is matched with the extended range of the Ranger autocannon, the *Rapier*'s weapons become vastly superior to those of other heavy fighters at long-range combat.

The *Chippewa* Class Fighter carries a wider variety of weapons than the *Rapier*, but the *Rapier* carries far greater armor protection. Twelve tons of PhilterMech myomer-weave armor plating makes the *Rapier* a favorite among green pilots who get a chance to handle larger craft. The *Rapier* can endure a great deal of punishment, and still have the firepower to continue in a long engagement.

[Editor's Note: The favorite defensive tactic of *Rapier* pilots was to keep the enemy at arm's length, as the range of the deadly Piledriver PPCs and Cavalier long-range missiles offer the craft its greatest advantage at long range. Defensively, the fighter followed the same tactics while flying in space. Often the *Rapier* was used to lure smaller fighters away from the battle and toward the planet. Once within the atmosphere, the *Rapier* used its superior turning abilities, pivoting around hard and using its PPCs to cripple the lighter craft. Enemy craft that tries to use superior speed to disengage found the long-range missiles cutting off their escape.

Captain McArthur Purvis Fullerton of the 2525th Independent AeroWing is the most famous *Rapier* pilot that never lived. He was a fictional character in the long-running holodrama, "Wings of Glory," who was known for his courage in combat. Though the character was fictional, the drama captured the popular imagination and raised the *Rapier*'s esteem, much to the satisfaction of Bauer Industries.]

Type: **RPR-100 Rapier**

Equipment		Mass
Engine:	AeroFord 340	27
Thrust	6	
Overthrust	9	
Structural Integrity:	9	
Heat Sinks:	12 (24)	2
Fuel:	75	5
Cockpit:		3
Armor Factor:	192+10	12
	Armor Value	
Cockpit	15	
Nose	45	
Left Wing	27	
Right Wing	27	
Fuselage	52	
Engine	36	

Weapons and Ammo:	Location	
AC/20	Nose	14
AMMO AC/20 (10)	Nose	2
PPC	Nose	7
PPC	Nose	7
LRM10	Fuselage	5
AMMO LRM 10 (12)	Fuselage	1

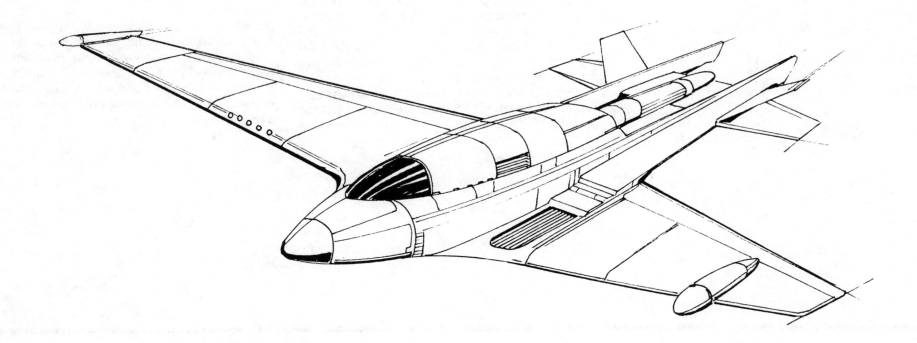

Mass: 90 tons
Frame: Wakazashi B3
Engine: PlasmaStar 270
Armor: Aerolight III
Armament:
   1 Thunderbolt 2C Large Laser
   1 Narc Missile Beacon
   2 Delta Dart-20 Long-Range Missile Racks
   2 Federated-6 Short-Range Missile Racks
   2 CeresArms Medium Lasers
Manufacturer: Harvard Company, Inc.
Communications System: MyComm LVR
Targeting and Tracking System: Artron 7

Overview:

The heaviest AeroSpace Fighter ever produced, the *Ahab* is sometimes billed as a highly mobile missile platform. It is intended for use against heavily entrenched positions.

A sound design, the *Ahab* has been modified only once since its introduction in 2697. Six years later, the Narc Missile Launcher was added to its weapons systems. Though this decreased the craft's firepower somewhat, proponents of the Narc convinced Star League commanders that the greater accuracy of the Narc would make the *Ahab* more lethal. They argued that this more than offsets the loss of the more powerful Starcutter D 1280.

Capabilities:

The *Ahab*'s fifteen and one-half tons of standard armor provide good protection, but, as with all Aero-Space Fighters, the rear quarter is the least well-protected. A pilot once compared the *Ahab*'s speed to "a moose in molasses," referring to the fact that the 270-rated engine does not provide the craft with much acceleration. At only fourteen and one-half tons, the engine makes up for this defect by leaving much extra space for additional weaponry.

Using its long-range missiles, the *Ahab* can begin firing at extreme range and continue the fight to close quarters. The bulk of the craft's firepower consists of two Delta Dart LRM 20s mounted on each wing. The missile storage packs are housed just underneath the launchers. They are filled with three tons of ammunition each. This sizable missile bay provides the *Ahab* with increased staying power, making it viable for prolonged conflict. Two Federated-6 short-range missiles are mounted inboard for short-range punch. When the missile supply is exhausted, or when the pilot closes on a target, the *Ahab* can depend on its single Thunderbolt large laser in the nose. Designers compensated for the *Ahab*'s poor maneuverability with twin, rear-mounted CeresArms medium lasers.

The Narc Missile Beacon, mounted in the nose, fires the Narc Pod, a magnetic missile with a powerful homing device, just behind its head. When attached to a target, the device emits a powerful homing signal that will draw any missile launched at the target. Pinpoint missile accuracy is possible with the Narc, allowing concentration of firepower on one target area and diminishing enemy Fighters' life expectancy.

[Editor's Note: The prototype of the *Ahab* did not utilize Narc Missile Pods. Instead, it mounted three medium lasers and four additional heat sinks. This early *Ahab* was not as fearsome in initial stages of engagement, but its additional medium lasers let it remain in a fight far longer once its missiles were exhausted.]

Type: **AHB-443 Ahab**

Equipment		Mass
Engine:	PlasmaStar 270	14.5
Thrust	5	
Overthrust	8	
Structural Integrity:	9	
Heat Sinks:	14	4
Fuel:	75	5
Cockpit:		3
Armor Factor:	248+10	15.5

	Armor Value
Cockpit	16
Nose	62
Left Wing	43
Right Wing	43
Fuselage	64
Engine	30

Weapons and Ammo:	Location	
Large Laser	Nose	5
Narc Beacon	Nose	3
Narc Pods-12	Nose	4
LRM20	Right Wing	10
AMMO LRM 20 (18)	Right Wing	3
LRM20	Left Wing	10
AMMO LRM 20 (18)	Left Wing	3
SRM6	Right Wing	3
AMMO SRM 6 (15)	Right Wing	1
SRM 6	Left Wing	3
AMMO SRM 6 (15)	Left Wing	1
Medium Laser	Rear	1
Medium Laser	Rear	1

VEHICLES

GABRIEL

Mass: 5 tons
Movement Type: Hover
Power Plant: VOX 35
Cruising Speed: 162 kph
Flank Speed: 243 kph
Armor: Bowie Ferro-Aluminum
Armament:
    1 Maxell TR Medium Laser
Manufacturer: Bowie Industries
Communications System: CBR CommStat
Targeting and Tracking System: Halo 901

Overview:

Riding a cushion of air, the fusion-powered Gabriel is easily the Star League's fastest ground vehicle. Lightning speed and excellent maneuverability have made the vehicle the standard scout of the Star League Defense Forces.

The thin armor hides the Gabriel's impressive features. Designed as an experiment by a team of aerospace engineers in 2712, the Gabriel surprised its designers with its apparent viability. The vice president of Bowie Industries submitted the plans to the Quartermaster Command, which was skeptical. Though a radical departure from standard design, the Gabriel was based on the cutting edge of aerospace technology. The Bowie engineers had spared no expense in making their toy a technological marvel. When the Quartermaster Command began to test the prototype, the armor crews could not adjust to the change in components, and so AeroSpace Fighter crews tested the machine.

Capabilities:

Though designed for reconnaissance and not combat, the Gabriel does carry a medium laser, the Maxell TR. Bowie's design drafts show that the engineers included the weapon and mounted it in a turret because they were "intrigued with the possibilities of a weapon with a 360-degree arc of fire." The automatic target-acquisition system is similar to those on AeroSpace Fighters. The turret swivels toward the closest threat, leaving it to the pilot to aim at a certain part and then fire. The pilot can override the system, but the logic algorithms have proven very successful.

The Gabriel carries Ferro-Aluminum armor, which is normally reserved for AeroSpace Fighters. This type of armor consists of a porous "foamed" alloy that is very hard but that is brittle compared to standard armor plate. Attached in tiles, the plating has proven successful on fighter designs. The Gabriel carries only one ton of the armor, not enough to stop even one medium laser hit on the side. The front, back, and turret have somewhat better protection.

The main purpose of the Gabriel is to gather intelligence, usually carrying information back to the parent unit. The Gabriel does carry the CBR CommStat system, advanced communications and sensor equipment for longer-range transmission. The communications pack scrambles the message and bounces it off the nearest satellite. Automatic satellite-tracking gear makes the process of sending and receiving messages quick and accurate. The only drawback is that the craft must slow to 100 kph to send or receive messages.

Pilots accidentally discovered how to angle the forward fans at such a degree so that pitch-back noise would make the Gabriel emit the sound of a wailing trumpet. To produce the trumpet sound makes the ride extremely rough. The practice is discouraged, but it remains a favorite method of announcing a pilot's return to the garrison.

Type: **Gabriel**

Equipment		Mass
Internal Structure:		0.5
Engine:	VOX 35	1.5
Type:	Fusion	
Cruise Speed:	15	
Flank Speed:	23	
Heat Sinks:	10	0
Control Equipment:		0.25
Lift Equipment:		0.5
Power Amplifier		0
Turret:		0.1
Armor Factor:	18	1

	Armor Value
Front	5
Left Side	3
Right Side	3
Rear	3
Turret	4

Weapons and Ammo:	Location	
Medium Laser	Turret	1

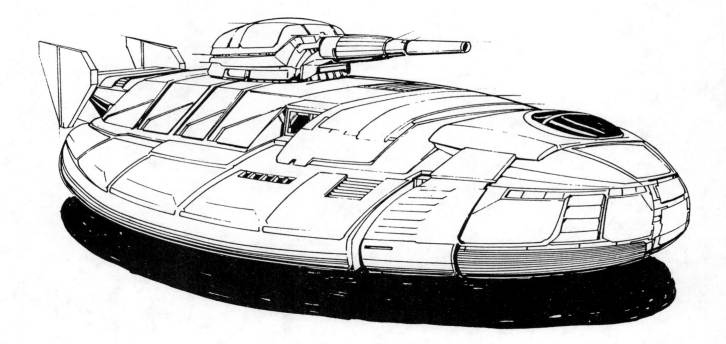

Mass: 10 tons
Movement Type: VTOL
Power Plant: Omni 70
Cruising Speed: 130 kph
Flank Speed: 194 kph
Armor: Aldis Heavy Ferro-Fibrous
Armament:
　　2 Omicron 950 Medium Lasers
Manufacturer: Aldis Industries
Communications System: Datacom 100
Targeting and Tracking System: Tarmac Quasar V

Overview:

The Ripper grew out of the Star League's need for a VTOL aircraft that could carry a squad of men and equipment into a battle and emerge intact. Design specifications issued in 2680 called for a craft with quick response and reliability, using proven components.

The Ripper normally carries elite infantry units and jump infantry squads, which need quick deployment or retrieval. The Ripper is so fast and maneuverable that the infantry compartment has special acceleration couches to handle the high Gs. The Ripper has fusion power, part of the vehicle's high price tag, and Ferro-Fibrous armor. Though this is not standard for VTOLs, special armor has made the Ripper stable and strong enough to endure the stresses created by eager pilots.

Capabilities:

Though heavily armored for a VTOL, the Ripper cannot survive against the firepower of a 'Mech or even a well-equipped infantry squad. A small laser can down the craft with two shots.

When the Ripper begins its descent, its twin lasers fire around the fringes of the landing zone. The pilot keeps his speed high for as long as possible. When the Ripper reaches the landing zone, the pilot pitches the rotor forward, slamming the throttle full open. This air brake sends loose components flying, but the tactic reduces the time the aircraft is exposed to enemy fire. The pilot slams the craft down, cutting the rotors for ten seconds. The engineer, who rides in the infantry compartment, hustles the squad out the door, throwing equipment after the departing soldiers. In seconds, the engineer is strapping himself back in as the craft prepares to take off. The pilot usually angles to the left, tilting the craft to spill any remaining pieces of equipment or lingering infantrymen. Once airborne, the pilot again fires the lasers as the craft quickly gains altitude.

Type: **Ripper**

Equipment		Mass
Internal Structure:		
Engine:	Omni 70	3
Type:	Fusion	
Cruise Speed:	12	
Flank Speed:	18	
Heat Sinks:	10	0
Control Equipment:		0.5
Rotor Tonnage:		1
Power Amplifier		0.2
Armor Factor:	27	1.5
	Armor	
	Value	
Front	10	
Left Side	5	
Right Side	5	
Rear	5	
Rotor	2	

Weapons and Ammo:	Location	
Medium Laser	Front	1
Medium Laser	Front	1

BEAGLE

Mass: 15 tons
Movement Type: Hover
Power Plant: Nissan 95
Cruising Speed: 130 kph
Flank Speed: 194 kph
Armor: Yelm 2.5 Ferro-Fibrous
Armament:
    1 Aberdovey Mk II Medium Laser
    1 Exostar-2C Small Laser
Manufacturer: Numall Armored Vehicles
Communications System: Essex 88
Targeting and Tracking System: Beagle Active
    Probe

Overview:

The development of the Beagle Active Probe gave BattleMechs an even greater advantage over vehicles and infantry. Not only were the other branches overmatched by the 'Mech, they also had nowhere to hide from this sophisticated sensor system. In 2666, the Star League Quartermaster Command authorized a contract with Numall Armored Vehicles for construction of the Beagle Hover-Scout.

The Beagle's main function was to carry the Active Probe into combat to give a tank or hover unit better information.

The hover vehicle was completed within twelve months, and soon deployed widely. After the initial shipments, however, crews discovered a malfunction in the turret ring. Quickly reversing the turret's direction caused it to lock, freezing the medium laser and sensor wand. Field repairs proved impossible, and Numall Armored Weapons of New Earth recalled the entire batch. Factory repairs often took as long as the original construction, and many tank units "forgot" to return their Beagles for adjustments. Though almost every SLDF tank unit has a Beagle, more than half are the original version and therefore subject to jamming turrets.

[Editor's Note: The Beagle remained prone to breakdown, and the vehicle disappeared during the First Succession War, more from mechanical difficulties than battlefield casualties.]

Capabilities:

Once the malfunction in the turret was corrected, the Beagle became an effective military vehicle. Never intended for heavy combat, its weapons were designed to discourage close inspection and provide the crew with an opportunity to escape. The design concept intended that the Beagle would be able to identify any enemy and flee before facing fire. In practice, however, a Beagle must often weather a sustained barrage after closing to gather information about the enemy. Though the Beagle carries three and one-half tons of Ferro-Fibrous plating, the armor provides only partial protection. With its speed, the Beagle is an elusive target that can usually make good its escape after completing its task. Almost every tank and hover company has one Beagle attached as a support vehicle.

A directional wand housed in the turret carries the sensors for the Active Probe. The Aberdovey Mk II medium laser that links directly to the Active Probe is noted for its accuracy. The Beagle mounts an Exostar-2C small laser to deal with infantry.

Type: **Beagle**

Equipment		Mass
Internal Structure:		1.5
Engine:	Nissan 95	4.5
Type:	Fusion	
Cruise Speed:	12	
Flank Speed:	18	
Heat Sinks:	10	0
Control Equipment:		0.75
Lift Equipment:		1.5
Power Amplifier		0
Turret:		0.25
Armor Factor:	63	3.5

	Armor Value
Front	15
Left Side	12
Right Side	12
Rear	10
Turret	14

Weapons and Ammo:	Location	
Beagle Probe	Turret	1.5
Medium Laser	Turret	1
Small Laser	Front	0.5

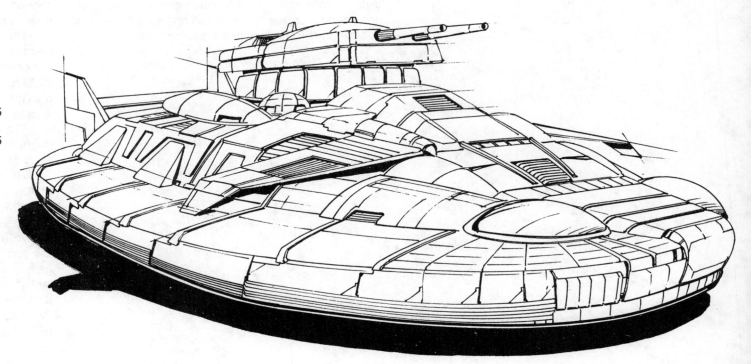

ROTUNDA

Mass: 20 tons
Movement Type: Wheeled
Power Plant: LTV 160
Cruising Speed: 97 kph
Flank Speed: 146 kph
Armor: Mercury Weave Ferro-Fibrous
Armament:
1 Holly SRM-2 Launcher
1 Amdecker 300 Large Laser
Manufacturer: Buhallin Military Products
Communications System: SP/2 HAYOT
Targeting and Tracking System: Hanover Sight
3000-A-K-P

Overview:

The Rotunda RND-J-111 is essentially a self-sufficient home and fighting vehicle for its one-person crew. It can operate for extended periods of time with little maintenance or other support. Its fusion power plant gives it unlimited range, allowing it to fill the role of scouting and recon duty for the Star League on Periphery worlds.

What separates the Rotunda from many Star League scout vehicles is that it is designed for a single driver/gunner who is not tied to the apron strings of a support crew. These sturdy vehicles usually operate in large numbers behind enemy lines. Their primary mission is to monitor enemy communications and troop movements, but they have enough firepower and speed to create havoc. In this role as raider/recon vehicle, the Rotunda is in a class by itself.

Capabilities:

The designers at Buhallin Military Products produced two models before the J-111 series. The J-100 Series, introduced in 2717, lacked a sturdy suspension system and needed frequent maintenance. The J-110 resolved the suspension difficulties, with only subtle changes in armor placement and engine shielding. The J-111 is a breakthrough in the technology of armored scouting cars.

The single-man Rotunda maximizes the comfort of the driver. It has ample storage for several week's worth of food and water, as well as all necessary tools and equipment for survival. A portable stove, tent, and survival gear are standard on the Rotunda. The cockpit can carry a passenger, but extra gear or the driver's personal effects often fill this space.

The sleek Rotunda often shows up on identification profiles as a civilian ICE transport instead of an armored scout car. Many 'Mechs manufactured since 2735 have modified their programming to recognize the Rotunda, but there are still large numbers of older 'Mechs that cannot.

The control and cockpit components protect the driver in combat, but this placement prevents quick entry and exit from the cockpit.

The RND-J-111 carries a Holly SRM-2 pack and an Amdecker 300 large laser. The Holly system is one of the best-known and most-trusted missile systems ever created. The Amdecker 300 large laser is less known, and some technicians have difficulty repairing the equipment. Drivers say the weapon sometimes generates heat unpredictably and thus causes difficulties in monitoring and adequately venting it. This heat buildup can damage the weapon and its mounting, forcing early maintenance. Still, the system is respected for its accuracy.

Type: **Rotunda**

Equipment		Mass		Weapons and Ammo:	Location	
Internal Structure:		2		Large Laser	Front	5
Engine:	LTV 160	9		SRM 2	Front	1
Type:	Fusion			AMMO SRM 2 (50)	Body	1
Cruise Speed:	9					
Flank Speed:	14					
Heat Sinks:	10	0				
Control Equipment:		1				
Lift Equipment:		0				
Power Amplifier		0				
Turret:		0				
Armor Factor:	18	1				

	Armor Value
Front	6
Left Side	4
Right Side	4
Rear	4

NIGHTSHADE

Mass: 25 tons
Movement Type: VTOL
Power Plant: Vlar 205
Cruising Speed: 130 kph
Flank Speed: 194 kph
Armor: FiberTech Light
Armament:
  1 Randall Medium Laser
Manufacturer: Yelm Weapons
Communications System: Johnston VRR
Targeting and Tracking System: NIRAD 210

Overview:

Though it is classified as a combat scout VTOL craft, the Nightshade's main function is to carry the Guardian ECM Suite into combat.

The Guardian emits a broad-band signal that interferes with all sonar, radar, UV, IR, and magscan sensors. This signal projects a "cloak" to a radius of 180 meters, protecting all units within the circle.

Enemy long-range sensors can find vehicles and 'Mechs within the curtain, but the Guardian obscures the reading, preventing identification. By the time the enemy gets within visual range, sensors can sometimes override the jamming, but most pilots rely on their own eyes.

The Nightshade, designed in 2597, was the first craft to carry the Guardian system.

Capabilities:

As a combat chopper, the Nightshade is mediocre. The massive engine gives the Nightshade excellent acceleration, but at the cost of cargo space.

The only weapon on the Nightshade is a medium laser mounted on the nose of the craft. The laser has an excellent service record and is hooked to the pilot's helmet. When the pilot turns his head, the gun swivels with him. It is a good system, but the Nightshade needs supporting weapons. The Nightshade carries only two tons of standard armor plating, and so it is vulnerable to even light ground fire. As with any VTOL, the pilot's main concern is the vulnerable rotor assembly, which cannot be effectively armored for aerodynamic reasons.

Type: **Nightshade**

Equipment		Mass
Internal Structure:		
Engine:	Vlar 205	12.75
Type:	Fusion	
Cruise Speed:	12	
Flank Speed:	18	
Heat Sinks:	10	0
Control Equipment:		1.25
Rotor Tonnage:		2.5
Power Amplifier		0.1
Armor Factor:	32	2
	Armor	
	Value	
Front	10	
Left Side	5	
Right Side	5	
Rear	8	
Rotor	2	

Weapons and Ammo:	Location	
Guardian ECM Suite	Body	1.5
Medium Laser	Front	1

CYRANO

Mass: 30 tons
Movement Type: VTOL
Power Plant: DAV 220
Cruising Speed: 130 kph
Flank Speed: 194 kph
Armor: Paulina DL Ferro-Fibrous
Armament:
1 Fuersturm-C Large Laser
Manufacturer: Paulina Weapons
Communications System: Garret M250
Targeting and Tracking System: Sky Tracer WL

Overview:

The heaviest VTOL in the Star League Defense Forces, the Cyrano is the standard gunship. Developed in 2622 to provide inexpensive support for ground troops, the Cyrano proved to be an able attack fighter. It also escorts the Ripper and the Nightshade on dangerous missions.

Besides its attack capabilities, the Cyrano carries the Beagle Active Probe to locate enemy infantry, armor, and 'Mechs.

Capabilities:

The dominant physical feature of the Cyrano is the forward-mounted Fuersturm-C large laser. The entire system weighs almost five tons and takes up the bulk of the forward section of the craft. It is this weapon that gave the craft its name and distinctive flying profile.

Because the weight is not balanced, Cyrano pilots must fly numerous training missions before they enter combat. These training sessions are vital to acquaint the pilots with the craft's unusual handling characteristics. To control the laser, the pilot uses an early version of the neurohelmet. Impulses from the Beagle display in front of the pilot, who simply looks at the target and presses the trigger. The Sky Tracer target-acquisition computer makes automatic adjustments. The Beagle provides instant analysis of the target, including damage, weapon status, and probable response. The systems blend well, giving the Cyrano excellent fighting ability.

As with all VTOL craft, aerodynamics and weight problems make it virtually impossible to include adequate armor. Because of this, the Cyrano is vulnerable to enemy fire.

The Beagle Active Probe is the state-of-the-art sensor system. Not only does it function at a much longer range, but it can pierce the Guardian ECM devices. The Beagle's memory unit records an encoded account of every battle. Should the Beagle encounter the foe again, it instantly displays a detailed profile of the enemy. The unit can also replay any battle on the tactical display. The pilot can alter actual actions with the joystick to see the consequences of different tactics. This mentor system is extremely popular with the pilots.

Type: **Cyrano**

Equipment		Mass	Weapons and Ammo:	Location	
Internal Structure:			Beagle Probe	Front	1.5
Engine:	DAV 220	15	Large Laser	Front	5
Type:	Fusion				
Cruise Speed:	12				
Flank Speed:	18				
Heat Sinks:	10	0			
Control Equipment:		1.5			
Rotor Tonnage:		3			
Power Amplifier		0.5			
Armor Factor:	9	0.5			
	Armor Value				
Front	3				
Left Side	2				
Right Side	2				
Rear	1				
Rotor	1				

LIGHTNING

Mass: 35 tons
Movement Type: Hover
Power Plant: GM 210
Cruising Speed: 119 kph
Flank Speed: 178 kph
Armor: 3/Star Slab Ferro-Fibrous
Armament:
    2 Raker-IV Medium Pulse Lasers
    2 Maxima One Shot SRM-4 Launchers
Manufacturer: Curtiss Industries
Communications System: Century Model 770
Targeting and Tracking System: TGI 2331C/TGI
    F-190

Overview:

The Lightning is a lightweight, high-speed, hover strike craft designed in 2696 by Curtiss Industries under contract for Star League. The Lightning's design gives it a limited but important combat role. Carrying only light armor and weaponry, the Lightning is not well-equipped to engage in protracted fire-fight. The craft's agility and advanced fire-control system allow it to close at high speed, maneuver to a position of advantage, and fire its small but accurate array of short-range weaponry.

In this way, the Lightning can harass enemy forces, especially slow 'Mechs and vehicles. Commanders often organize teams of Lightnings into strike forces, employing them in the initial phases to break up enemy formations and to cause general confusion.

When used for other missions, the Lightning has many drawbacks. Not well-equipped to perform reconnaissance and too poorly armed and armored for more traditional combat, the Lightning can become a liability when its particular uses are unnecessary.

Capabilities:

The GM 210 engine gives the Lightning a maximum speed of more than 175 kph. To keep from crashing into trees and other terrain obstacles, the Lightning carries a special collision-avoidance radar and computer system that detects objects at a distance and adjusts the Lightning's heading and speed to avoid them. This system can hinder the vehicle in combat, and so the driver can override it.

The craft is extremely maneuverable, mostly because of special thrusters mounted at various points along the hovercraft's hull. These thrusters utilize the hovercraft's high pressure air system to assist the vehicle in maneuvering.

An interesting feature of the Lightning's sleek, low hull is a set of wings mounted near the rear. At high speeds, these wings provide added lift and stability. In fact, the wings have elevators that allow the fast-moving vehicle to jump over low obstacles. Moving at top speed, the hovercraft has been able to clear two-meter fences in tests. In practice, this is a difficult and dangerous maneuver attempted only by expert drivers.

Not designed for extended missions, the Lightning has a cramped crew compartment, a T-shaped area just large enough to hold the driver at the front and the gunner and commander side by side right behind him. This tiny crew compartment also limits the amount of personal gear and supplies that the vehicle can carry.

The Lightning is lightly armed with weapons designed for short-range combat, two Raker-IV medium pulse lasers, and two Maxima SRM-4 One Shot SRM launchers. These weapons can do extensive damage at close range.

Type: **Lightning**

Equipment		Mass
Internal Structure:		3.5
Engine:	GM 210	13.5
Type:	Fusion	
Cruise Speed:	11	
Flank Speed:	17	
Heat Sinks:	10	0
Control Equipment:		1.75
Lift Equipment:		3.5
Power Amplifier		0
Turret:		0
Armor Factor:	63	3.5

	Armor Value
Front	20
Left Side	16
Right Side	16
Rear	11

Weapons and Ammo:	Location	
Medium Pulse Laser	Front	2
Medium Pulse Laser	Front	2
Medium Machine Gun		.5
Ammo MG (100)		.5
SRM 4 (OS)	Right	2.5
SRM 4 (OS)	Left	2.5

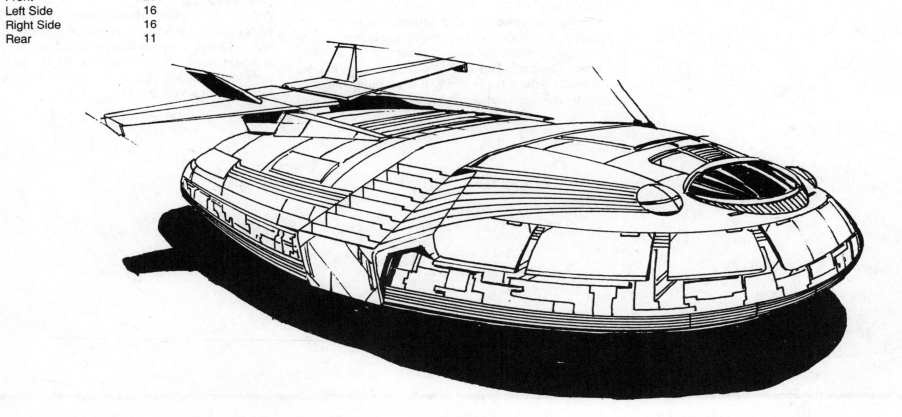

ZEPHYR

Mass: 40 tons
Movement Type: Hover
Power Plant: GM 185
Cruising Speed: 97 kph
Flank Speed: 146 kph
Armor: Grumman CRT Ferro-Fibrous
Armament:
   3 Sorenstein IV Medium Lasers
   1 Shannon SRM-6 Launcher
   1 Harmon Small Laser
Manufacturer: Grumman Industries
Communications System: Guardian ECM Suite
Targeting and Tracking System: AlloranTarget
   Acquisition Gear

Overview:

As originally designed in 2620, the Zephyr was to be a medium duty hover tank with the capability of supporting infantry units and responding quickly to fill gaps in the line. While the Quartermaster Command was considering the design, the SLDF was looking for a way to set ambushes with the new and successful Chaparral missile tank. The new Guardian ECM System showed promise, but its carrier, the Nightshade, was too flimsy to keep company with medium tanks and its exceptional speed was unnecessary. The generals of the Quartermaster Command sent the Zephyr design back to Grumman Industries with orders to install the Guardian.

Capabilities:

Though designed as a fast response tank, the Zephyr has taken on the role of screening friendly vehicles, usually including Chaparrals, by jamming enemy sensors. The Zephyr's armor plating is adequate to defend the jamming device, but commanders try to keep it out of combat because its firepower is not powerful enough to justify risking the expensive Guardian equipment.

The three medium lasers provide the main attack, with the short-range missile system normally deployed to deal with close threats or to clear a path for the vehicle. The two systems work well together, providing a good weapons mix for the hover tank. The small laser, mounted in the rear of the vehicle, provides some cover when the Zephyr is fleeing the field. The main weakness of the weapons system is the lack of long-range power.

The Guardian system is a broad-band jamming device that obscures sonar, radar, UV, IR, and magscan readings. The device creates a 180-meter radius electronic cloud that secretes the sensor profiles of everything within.

[Editor's Note: The original version of the Zephyr without the Guardian device was produced in limited numbers. The vehicle mounted an additional 2-Pack short-range missile launcher and 50 rounds of missiles facing the rear. It also carried an additional half ton of armor on the front.]

Type: **Zephyr**

Equipment		Mass
Internal Structure:		4
Engine:	GM 185	11.25
Type:	Fusion	
Cruise Speed:	9	
Flank Speed:	13.5	
Heat Sinks:	10	0
Control Equipment:		2
Lift Equipment:		4
Power Amplifier		0
Turret:		0.4
Armor Factor:	125	7

	Armor Value
Front	29
Left Side	24
Right Side	24
Rear	19
Turret	29

Weapons and Ammo:	Location	
Medium Laser	Turret	1
Medium Laser	Turret	1
Medium Laser	Turret	1
TAG	Turret	1
SRM 6	Front	3
AMMO SRM 6 (30)	Body	2
Small Laser	Rear	0.5
Guardian ECM Suite	Body	1.5

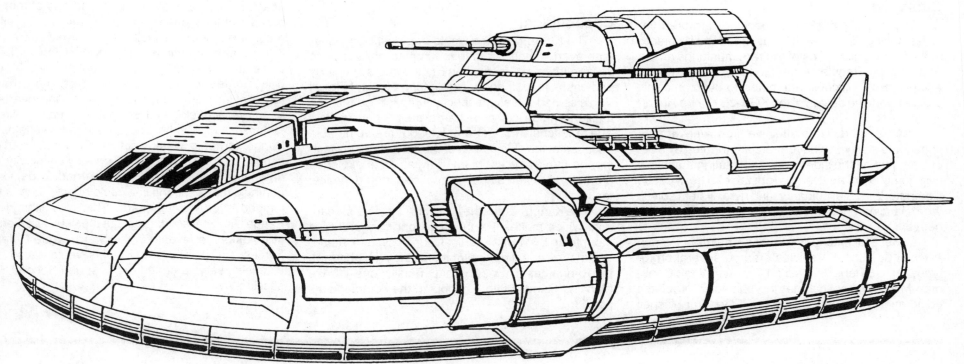

Mass: 50 tons
Movement Type: Hover/Jump
Power Plant: VOX 165
Cruising Speed: 86 kph
Flank Speed: 130 kph
Jump Jets: Mitchell JB Thrust Bottles
   Jump Capacity: 180 meters
Armor: Durolex
Armament:
   1 Lonworth Type V Autocannon
   1 General Datatech Vertical Launch LRM-10
      System
   1 General Datatech Vertical Launch SRM-4
      System
   1 Tri-Axe Machine Gun
Manufacturer: Mitchell Vehicles
Communications System: Stony AIX
Targeting and Tracking System: AL2200

Overview:

One of the biggest drawbacks of armored vehicles facing BattleMechs has been their inferior mobility and agility. One of the rare mustangs on the Star League Regular Army General Staff, General Alvarez "Bull" Mitchell, attempted to overcome this problem with the design of the KGA-2B Kanga Hover/Jump Tank.

The Kanga delivers effective firepower with the speed and agility of a hovercraft, augmented by a set of jump jets on the sides of its keel plating that allow it to jump over any terrain obstacle. The AL2200 Computer's inertial guidance and gyro system solves the balancing problems inherent in hover/jump maneuvers.

At General Mitchell's request, Chairman Ramon Mitchell of Mitchell Vehicles ordered several prototypes built. Extensive trials on Graham IV left Chairman Mitchell skeptical that the balancing problems could ever be solved. A frustrated General Mitchell staked his large personal fortune on further research and then full production, which began in mid-2650.

The Kanga became one of the most successful vehicles of the Star League's Regular Army. The jump jets did improve the tank's abilities, though the vehicle could not hope to rival any BattleMech.

In the Kanga's first 100 years, 27,000 of these useful vehicles have been built at Mitchell Vehicles. [EDITOR'S NOTE: Even today, a Kanga occasionally shows up on the battlefield, but without its jumping ability because components for the sophisticated AL2200 Computer have been unavailable for at least a century. Almost all of the 50 or so remaining Kangas are simply hovertanks now. A handful, however, have lost their ability to hover but have kept their jump jets operational. These oddities are pure "jump tanks," with that as their only mobility on the battlefield. Despite the great surprise factor, these orphans have little value in a pitched battle.]

Capabilities:

The KGA-2B Kanga would be an efficient hover tank even without its unique jumping abilities. The Janzen Internal Combustion Engine offers simplicity and ease of repair and replacement, though Mitchell Vehicles had to design special jump jets so that the Janzen engine could recharge their thrust bottles. These Mitchell JBs perform well but are vulnerable because of the skimpiness of the side armor protecting the thrust bottles. Many Kangas have exploded prematurely when a chance shot penetrated the fuel tanks.

The Kanga carries the Lonworth Type V Autocannon, which makes it a threat at long range. It also mounts an LRM/SRM vertical launch system imbedded in the central portion of the body. With no turret, the Kanga has a low silhouette. Finally, one Tri-Axe Machine Gun fits into a cupola in the commander's position.

The Durolex armor is adequate in most respects, but weakness on the sides of the main body are the Kanga's biggest drawback. Several design changes to eliminate the problem failed, all because the thrust bottles occupy too much room.

The AL2200 Computer is part of the sophisticated so-called Artificial Intelligence series developed by the Nirasaki Computers Collective on Caph. It automatically handles all routine functions, including gyro-stability during jumps and hover-maneuver. The AL2200 can operate the vehicle independently on a preprogrammed mission.

The Kanga's targeting and tracking system is second to none. Manual CDC components are slaved to the AL2200 Computer, allowing the simultaneous targeting of up to four enemy vehicles or installations, even during complicated jump maneuvers or evasive tactics.

The Kanga appears in units throughout the Star League. Usually deployed in squadrons of four vehicles, Kangas often remain in reserve for either reconnaissance or assault missions in difficult terrain. Kangas also sometimes support 'Mech lances, being one of the few vehicles that can match a 'Mech's mobility. Some shortsighted commanders ignore the potential of the Kanga and use it as a normal hovertank.

Tactical doctrine for using Kanga units is similar to that for light 'Mechs. The jump maneuver helps the Kanga target a weak spot in an enemy vehicle, usually the rear. This tactic worked well initially, but defending commanders soon learned to deploy in depth so that a second line could attack Kangas that jumped over the vanguard. This ploy limited the Kanga's tactical advantage, but the vehicle's mobility still makes it a favorite in the Star League Defense Forces. [EDITOR'S NOTE: This vehicle also saw extensive service during the First and Second Succession Wars.]

Type: **Kanga**

Equipment		Mass	Weapons and Ammo:	Location	
Internal Structure:		5	AC/5	Front	8
Engine:	VOX 165	12	AMMO LRM 5 (24)	Body	1
Type:	I.C.E.		LRM10	Body	5
Cruise Speed:	8		AMMO LRM 10 (12)	Body	1
Flank Speed:	12		SRM 4	Body	2
Jumping MP:	6		AMMO SRM 4 (25)	Body	1
			MG Body	0.5	
Heat Sinks:	0	0	AMMO MG (200)	Body	1
Control Equipment:		2.5	Jump Jets	Body	3
Lift Equipment:		5			
Power Amplifier		0			
Turret:		0			
Armor Factor:	56	3.5			

	Armor Value
Front	20
Left Side	12
Right Side	12
Rear	12
Turret	0

Mass: 50 tons
Movement Type: Tracked
Power Plant: Nissan 200
Cruising Speed: 43 kph
Flank Speed: 65 kph
Armor: 1/Star Slab
Armament:
    2 Sapphire Medium Lasers
    1 Shrike SRM-6 Launcher
    2 AIL Arrow IV Launchers
Manufacturer: Grumman Industries
Communications System: TransComm 12
Targeting and Tracking System: TransComm
    WDS40A

Overview:

The Chaparral is a tracked missile tank introduced in 2611 to serve among mobile units where self-propelled Long Toms and Snipers could not travel. The Chaparral fills its role well and continues to serve with front-line units. Though the vehicle's heavy firepower has made it popular, its weapons have somewhat shorter range than traditional artillery guns, forcing the Chaparral to operate near the front lines.

Capabilities:

The Chaparral's main armament is the Arrow IV surface-to-surface missile system, which consists of two launchers mounted in pods that are elevated just before firing. Afterward, they lower to their normal positions, giving the Chaparral a low profile. The Arrow IV missiles come in two main varieties, those that home in on signals from Target Acquisition Gear (TAG) and those that explode with general damage over a wider area. These missiles, especially the homing types, are much more expensive than equally destructive rounds for Long Toms, Snipers, or Thumpers. The Chaparral complements infantry and light armored units because it need not be in the immediate zone of combat. All that is necessary is that a vehicle with a TAG system designate a target. Within seconds, an Arrow IV missile will strike the target with deadly accuracy.

When an enemy gets too close, the Chaparral has a small array of defensive weapons to keep the foe at bay. This weaponry consists of two Sapphire medium lasers mounted on the sides of the hull and a rear-firing Shrike SRM-6 missile launcher. These weapons concentrate firepower in the vehicle's rear arc, reflecting the fact that the Chaparral fights at close range only in retreat.

The Chaparral's moderate amount of armor reflects the same fact, with most on the sides and back. With a total of 5.5 tons of armor, the vehicle survives most close encounters.

The vehicle carries a four-man crew, consisting of a driver, gunner, radio operator, and tank commander. The large armored cab just forward of the missile launcher houses all four. The fusion engine precludes fuel problems, giving the missile tank the capacity to operate for extended periods of combat. Chaparrals also have a good service record, with a low breakdown rate.

Type: **Chaparral**

Equipment		Mass
Internal Structure:		5
Engine:	Nissan 200	12.75
Type:	Fusion	
Cruise Speed:	4	
Flank Speed:	6	
Heat Sinks:	10	0
Control Equipment:		2.5
Lift Equipment:		0
Power Amplifier		0
Turret:		0
Armor Factor:	88	5.5
	Armor Value	
Front	16	
Left Side	18	
Right Side	18	
Rear	36	

Weapons and Ammo:	Location	
Medium Laser	Right	1
Medium Laser	Left	1
SRM 6	Rear	3
AMMO SRM 6 (15)	Body	1
Arrow IV	Front	15
Ammo Arrow IV (15)	Body	3

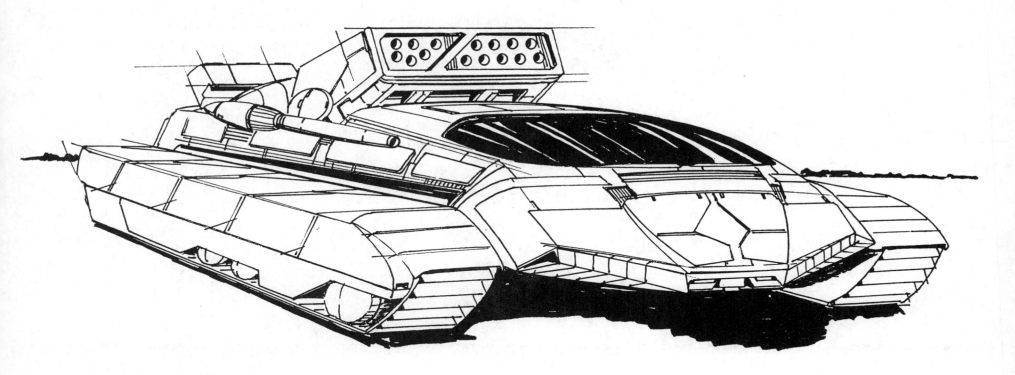

THOR

Mass: 55 tons
Movement Type: Wheeled
Power Plant: Strand 255
Cruising Speed: 54 kph
Flank Speed: 81 kph
Armor: Ulston105 Ferro-Fibrous, CASE
Armament:
    1 Thumper Artillery Piece
    2 Magna LT Medium Lasers
Manufacturer: Ulston Armor
Communications System: RedStar III
Targeting and Tracking System: TBR LaserTrac

Overview:

To fill the need for quick artillery response on a fluid battlefield, the Star League Defense Forces commissioned a vehicle to carry the Thumper Artillery Piece at speeds of 80 kilometers per hour on flat terrain.

The Quartermaster Command chose the Thor as the final design for two reasons. It was the fastest design submitted, and the only one that met the 80 kph specification. It also provided the most protection for its crew. Though its exterior armor is not exceptional, the Thor's CASE system for ammunition storage guards against internal shell explosions. Some members of the Quartermaster Command balked at a wheeled vehicle as too limited in some terrain, but the Thor's advantages outweighed this concern. Production began in 2680.

Capabilities:

Though the Thor carries a respectable amount of Ferro-Fibrous armor, today's weapons are so powerful that the Thor often relies on its speed for defense. The vehicle cannot fire when on the move, but setting up the firing station requires less than one minute. The vehicle can move again in 30 seconds.

Though the lightest artillery piece used by the Star League, the Thumper has excellent range and a good rate of fire. Employed in quantity, Thumper groups can level a city block in a matter of minutes. The trans-optical aiming system, which links the spotter to the artillery piece, contains some of the most advanced communications equipment in existence.

The Thor carries twin medium lasers in its turret, allowing the vehicle to offer some resistance if the enemy gets close. The lasers are powerful enough to provide some defense, but not enough to give the Thor crew any ideas of prolonging an engagement.

The Cellular Ammunition Storage Equipment on the Thor provides excellent crew protection in the event of an ammunition explosion. The shell storage compartment is lined with slabs of Ferro-Fibrous plating on five sides. Should the compartment rupture, the heavier plating channels the explosion to the sixth side, which blows out the rear of the vehicle. Though the blast blows off the rear armor and cripples the vehicle, the crew normally survives.

Type: **Thor**

Equipment		Mass
Internal Structure:		5.5
Engine:	Strand 255	19.5
Type:	Fusion	
Cruise Speed:	5	
Flank Speed:	8	
Heat Sinks:	10	0
Control Equipment:		2.75
Lift Equipment:		0
Power Amplifier		0
Turret:		0.2
Armor Factor:	134	7.5

	Armor Value
Front	30
Left Side	25
Right Side	25
Rear	24
Turret	30

Weapons and Ammo:	Location	
Thumper Artillery Piece	Front	15
Thumper Ammo (40)	Body	2
CASE	Body	0.5
Medium Laser	Turret	1
Medium Laser	Turret	1

Mass: 60 tons
Movement Type: Wheeled
Power Plant: DAV 220
Cruising Speed: 43 kph
Flank Speed: 65 kph
Armor: PanzerSlab 2, CASE
Armament:
    1 M-7 Gauss Rifle
    2 Intek Medium Lasers
    1 Harpoon-6 SRM Launcher
Manufacturer: Leopard Armor of Terra
Communications System: Teledon 19
Targeting and Tracking System: Baltex K590

Overview:

The Demon has been the Star League's standard fighting vehicle for engaging 'Mechs since its introduction in 2716. With respectable maneuverability, good armor, and the powerful Gauss Rifle mounted in the turret, the Demon is a match for light and medium 'Mechs.

Normally assigned in pairs instead of the usual four-vehicle lance, Demons have been known to wait in ambush for days. When a target presents itself, the two vehicles burst from cover and charge toward the target. Fights are usually brief, but bloody. The boldness of the attack sometimes sends a 'Mech into flight.

Demon crews must be careful, however, not to give themselves away too soon. Speedy, light 'Mechs can gain the upper hand by getting behind the Demon, which was designed for frontal charges and so has little protection on its rear facing.

Capabilities:

Mounting ten tons of slab armor, the Demon is well-protected for its class. The armor is concentrated on the front of the vehicle, making the Demon a tough opponent when engaged in a head-on attack. The sides and turret carry a standard load of armor, but the back is much more lightly protected.

The Demon carries an excellent mix of weapons, the most powerful being the M-7 Gauss Rifle. Based on ancient Terran technology, the Gauss Rifle uses electromagnets to propel the shell down the barrel. This system builds up little heat, but it requires tremendous amounts of power and space. For these reasons, only heavy vehicles and 'Mechs normally carry the Gauss Rifle. The weapon provides excellent firepower, and the turret gives it a 360-degree field of fire. Two Intek medium lasers, mounted on the sides of the vehicle, and a forward-firing Harpoon-6 short-range missile system augment the Gauss Rifle. These systems are housed in the body of the Demon, providing excellent secondary fire against close-assault attacks. A Cellular Ammunition Storage Equipment system protects the missile loads.

[Editor's Note:The only Demon variant, named the Horned Demon, replaced the short-range missile launcher and CASE system with two additional forward-firing medium lasers and two extra heat sinks. The Horned Demon moved the medium lasers from the side to the front of the vehicle, providing excellent attack ability forward at the cost of side protection. Horned Demons were vulnerable in an open engagement and rarely deploy except in defensive positions.]

Type: **Demon**

Equipment		Mass
Internal Structure:		6
Engine:	DAV 220	15
Type:	Fusion	
Cruise Speed:	4	
Flank Speed:	6	
Heat Sinks:	10	0
Control Equipment:		3
Lift Equipment:		0
Power Amplifier		0
Turret:		1.5
Armor Factor:	160	10

	Armor Value
Front	50
Left Side	30
Right Side	30
Rear	20
Turret	30

Weapons and Ammo:	Location	
Gauss Rifle	Turret	15
Gauss Ammo (30)	Body	2
Medium Laser	Left	1
Medium Laser	Right	1
SRM 6	Front	3
AMMO SRM 6 (30)	Body	2
CASE	Body	0.5

Mass: 65 tons
Movement Type: Tracked
Power Plant: Magna 260
Cruising Speed: 43 kph
Flank Speed: 65 kph
Armor: Grumman CRT Ferro-Fibrous
Armament:
    1 Sniper Artillery Piece
    1 RAMTech 500 Large Laser
Manufacturer: Grumman Industries
Communications System: O/P GRD 300
Targeting and Tracking System: O/P GRD059

Overview:

With the success of the Thor Armored Fighting Vehicle, designers attempted to replace the Thumper with the heavier Sniper Artillery Piece. The weight of the Sniper forced them to abandon the Thor's chassis and to create a new carrier.

The resulting vehicle was much changed from the successful Thor. To support the weight and provide stability, designers used tracks instead of wheels. The designers sacrificed speed for additional armor and mounted a single RAMTech 500 large laser in the turret as the only secondary weapon. Field tests were acceptable, and production began in 2702.

The original vehicles arrived at their assigned units with faulty tread locks on the inner track wheels. When the vehicle operated at flank speed, the lock tended to slip and throw the tread. Designers quickly went back to the drawing board, but thousands of Marksmen had already come off the production lines. Newer models had no problems, but not all the initial vehicles were retrofitted. These vehicles continued to be problematic, and many on far-flung words simply fell into disuse. [EDITOR'S NOTE: These are the vehicles that have survived to the present. Not knowing of the improvements, we have considered the Marksman a worthless design. Most have had their fusion engines stripped out and the chasis and weapons cannibalized for spare parts.]

Capabilities:

Although considered a mobile artillery piece, the Marksman lacks speed. The tracks allow the vehicle to enter most terrain, but at the cost of speed. Because of the Marksman's inability to outrun its enemies, designers included extra armor, seven and one-half tons of Ferro-Fibrous armor, most of it concentrated in the front.

The Sniper is the standard medium-duty artillery piece of the Star League Defense Forces. Though its range is short for an artillery piece, the Sniper does more damage than most others. The Marksman's only secondary weapon is the large laser mounted in the turret. Tied into the sophisticated tracking system, the laser has a reputation of being extremely accurate, even at long range.

Because of the shorter range of the Sniper, the Marksman is more likely to see combat than other artillery pieces. Because of this, the Marksman carries a second fire-control computer, which controls the Sniper for direct fire. The additional computer allows the target tracking computers to lock onto a target much more quickly than normal, giving the Sniper notable direct-fire capabilities.

Type: **Marksman**

Equipment		Mass
Internal Structure:		6.5
Engine:	Magna 260	20.25
Type:	Fusion	
Cruise Speed:	4	
Flank Speed:	6	
Heat Sinks:	10	0
Control Equipment:		3.25
Lift Equipment:		0
Power Amplifier		0
Turret:		0.5
Armor Factor:	134	7.5

	Armor Value
Front	54
Left Side	20
Right Side	20
Rear	20
Turret	20

Weapons and Ammo:	Location	
Sniper Artillery Piece	Front	20
Sniper Ammo (20)	Body	2
Large Laser	Turret	5

MAGI

Mass: 70 tons
Movement Type: Tracked
Power Plant: Magna 350
Cruising Speed: 54 kph
Flank Speed: 81 kph
Armor: Killosh Xtra-Weave Ferro-Fibrous
Armament:
    3 Randall Hellbitch Medium Lasers
    2 Ramsey-65 Machine Guns
Manufacturer: Killosh Industries
Communications System: Hesperus 5GT
Targeting and Tracking System: Lynx RM

Overview:

A scandal early in the contract process nearly canceled Magi production before it started. Tempest Halloran, the beautiful chief executive of Killosh Industries, had a long and secret friendship with General Aaron Clavy of the Quartermaster Command. When the Star League Defense Forces issued the call for tank designs using Ferro-Fibrous armor, dozens of defense contractors submitted proposals.

After what many critics called summary consideration and no debate, the Quartermaster Command bestowed on Killosh Industries what became known as "the gift of the Magi." Six months later, General Clavy's friendship with Tempest Halloran came to light. Testing was halted, General Clavy was transferred to the Transport Command, and a full-blown investigation ensued.

An 18-month inquiry uncovered no wrongdoing or special treatment. Testing resumed, and Magi prototypes performed well. The critics fell silent, and the Magi entered full production in 2727. The Magi has become an effective anti-infantry vehicle. Though its lack of a turret gives it an odd appearance for an armored vehicle and it is less than effective against tanks, it fills an important role in the military and in dealing with civil unrest.

Capabilities:

The Magi mounts nine and one-half tons of Ferro-Fibrous armor, which was originally designed for BattleMechs. This armor has not been completely successful on the Magi, but it does provide more protection than other armor. Abrupt maneuvers have caused hair-line cracks between the plates, a problem engineers have been unable to remedy.

The Magi's main weapons are three Randall Hellbitch medium lasers, mounted to the front, left, and right. The system lacks the concentrated firepower of most tanks, but the fire-control system is among the most advanced in the Star League. With three independent target-acquisition computers, the Magi can fire in three directions at the same time. The Magi can thus engage a number of foes simultaneously, but it lacks the knockout punch needed against armored targets. The twin Ramsey-65 machine guns normally fire with the front laser.

The Cellular Ammunition Storage Equipment system houses the machine gun ammunition, protecting the storage racks with sheets of Ferro-Fibrous armor.

Type: **Magi**

Equipment		Mass
Internal Structure:		7
Engine:	Magna 350	44.25
Type:	Fusion	
Cruise Speed:	5	
Flank Speed:	8	
Heat Sinks:	10	0
Control Equipment:		3.5
Lift Equipment:		0
Power Amplifier		0
Turret:		0
Armor Factor:	170	9.5

	Armor Value
Front	44
Left Side	43
Right Side	43
Rear	40
Turret	0

Weapons and Ammo:	Location	
Medium Laser	Front	1
Medium Laser	Right	1
Medium Laser	Left	1
MG	Front	0.5
MG	Front	0.5
AMMO MG (200)	Body	1
CASE	Body	0.5

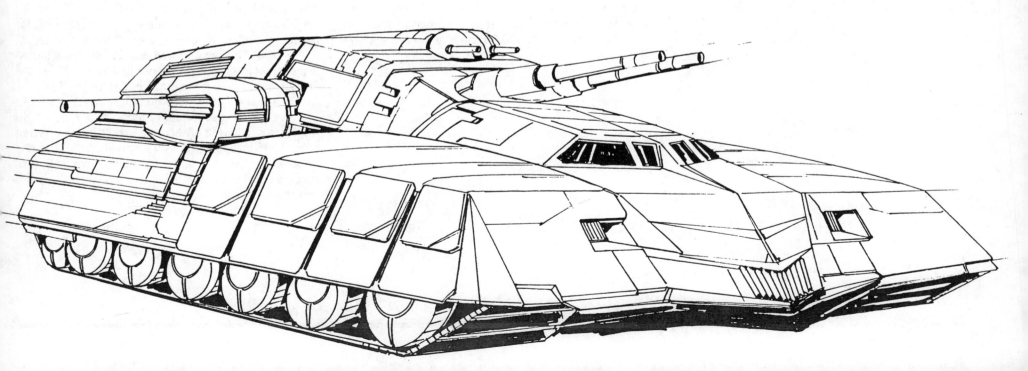

BURKE

Mass: 75 tons
Movement Type: Tracked
Power Plant: GM 150
Cruising Speed: 22 kph
Flank Speed: 32 kph
Armor: Acbar 55 Ferro-Fibrous
Armament:
   3 Chalker Model 25 Particle Cannon
   1 Holly-10 Long Range Missile Launcher
Manufacturer: Foretechno
Communications System: 1 Drivion 300
Targeting and Tracking System: Scope 30 RNDST

Overview:

Engineers at Foretechno designed the Burke for static defense against BattleMechs. Even the brashest 'Mech commanders are wary of the Burke. To make the vehicle capable of destroying a 'Mech, Foretechno engineers loaded it with weapons, at the expense of speed.

The designers succeeded in making the Burke a threat to all but the heaviest 'Mechs. The first Burke emerged from the assembly line in 2580, and Foretechno continued to crank them out for the next ten years. The Burke gained such a reputation that its enemies began to look for ways to avoid it. With its limited mobility, the Burke could not offer much in the way of pursuit ability. Garrison forces prized the Burke, but when front-line divisions began to shun it for its lack of flexibility, orders fell off.

Production at Foretechno has started up and then ceased again numerous times over the last 50 years. This uneven flow of contracts has caused financial problems for the contractor. Quartermaster Command analysts fear that Foretechno may go bankrupt, creating havoc for the maintenance of the thousands of Burkes in service.

Capabilities:.

The Burke can outshoot many BattleMechs of the same weight classification. The bulk of its firepower rests within the triple-mounted Chalker Model 25 PPC. Some 'Mechs have a classic "one-two punch," but none can match the triple blast from the Burke. Each weapon can have a different target, or they can fire in unison, making them a deadly combination in a firefight.

When all three PPCs hit at the same instant, they can overload a 'Mech's computer or cause enough electronic noise to jam communications or targeting data temporarily. Most Star League BattleMechs carry dampers to channel out such power bursts, but many in service to the member-states do not.

The Burke also carries a long-range missile system that has become known as a "Holly-Rack." The Holly-10 Long Range Missile Launcher, made by a contractor that has earned a spotless reputation, is one of the most powerful Holly has ever produced. When working in conjunction with the Scope 30 RNDST targeting and tracking system, it accounts for trajectory, ECM, atmospheric conditions, and target movement. The major drawback of the Burke's missile system is its limited number of reloads. Thus, the Holly-Rack is only a backup system for the PPCs.

The Burke's main weakness is its inability to hold up in a prolonged engagement. In a quick fight against a single BattleMech, it can hold its own. When faced with multiple opponents, however, the Burke is hobbled by its very strength, the concentration of firepower. The Burke's poor maneuverability worsens the problem.

Type: **Burke**

Equipment		Mass	Weapons and Ammo:	Location	
Internal Structure:		7.5	PPC	Turret	7
Engine:	GM 150	8.25	PPC	Turret	7
Type:	Fusion		PPC	Turret	7
Cruise Speed:	2		LRM10	Front	5
Flank Speed:	3		AMMO LRM 10 (12)	Body	1
Heat Sinks:	30	20			
Control Equipment:		3.75			
Lift Equipment:		0			
Power Amplifier		0			
Turret:		2.1			
Armor Factor:	108	6			

	Armor Value
Front	30
Left Side	20
Right Side	20
Rear	16
Turret	22

Mass: 80 tons
Movement Type: Tracked
Power Plant: Pitban 320
Cruising Speed: 43 kph
Flank Speed: 65 kph
Armor: PyroTec ArmorSlab
Armament:
    1M-9 Gauss Rifle
Manufacturer: Jolassa Armored Vehicles
Communications System: HIV-13
Targeting and Tracking System: Quadrant XD

Overview:

Jolassa Armored Vehicles designed the Fury in 2637 as a command vehicle for armor and infantry units. Commanders greeted the Fury with enthusiasm, largely because of its protection and weapon. The Quartermaster Command approved Jolassa's contract for sale of the Fury to League member-states, but without the advanced Nirasaki-400X Command Computer.

Despite the vehicle's high cost, orders for the Fury poured into Jolassa's headquarters on Tybalt. Thousands of computer-equipped models went out to SLDF commanders, and thousands of "dumb" versions went to the militaries of the Member States. [EDITOR'S NOTE: Only a handful of Furies survived the First Succession War. The opening months of the Second Succession War destroyed those that remained.]

Capabilities:

The Fury packs 15 tons of standard slab armor on a tracked chassis. Well-armored and solidly built, the Fury can withstand considerable abuse, from either the driver or the enemy. It also has excellent speed for its size.

The Fury's only weapon is the 1M-9 Gauss Rifle in the turret. The rifle gives the vehicle excellent weapon range and firepower, but the Fury lacks the ability to stop a close-assault attack. Original designs called for the addition of a medium laser on a second turret, but procurement officers considered the additional weapon unnecessary for a command vehicle. Though the Gauss Rifle is a powerful weapon, the system requires large amounts of shielding to protect the surrounding electronic components from the intense magnetic field.

The Nirasaki-400X Command Computer is the fastest battlefield computer in the Inner Sphere. Packed with six parallel processors, the 400X can easily monitor the battlefield operations of a battalion. When tied to the communications system of the Fury, the 400X tracks enemy troop movements, identifies suspected positions, and analyzes enemy goals. The system was very well received in prototype testing, but its complexity requires the assignment of an extra computer specialist to the battalion command staff. [Editor's Note: The only variant of the Fury, the Fury II, removed the Nirasaki Command Computer and one ton of Gauss ammunition. In the extra space, designers packed a forward-firing medium laser and half a ton of additional side armor. Usually deployed as a 'Mech hunter, the Fury II became increasingly popular with armor crews.]

Type: **Fury**

Equipment		Mass
Internal Structure:		8
Engine:	Pitban 320	33.75
Type:	Fusion	
Cruise Speed:	4	
Flank Speed:	6	
Heat Sinks:	10	0
Control Equipment:		4
Lift Equipment:		0
Power Amplifier		0
Turret:		1.5
Armor Factor:	240	15

	Armor Value
Front	60
Left Side	40
Right Side	40
Rear	40
Turret	60

Weapons and Ammo:	Location	
Gauss Rifle	Turret	15
Gauss Ammo (20)	Body	2

RHINO

Mass: 80 tons
Movement Type: Tracked
Power Plant: Pitban 240
Cruising Speed: 32 kph
Flank Speed: 49 kph
Armor: Pantherskin VII
Armament:
    2 Delta Dagger-20 LRM Launchers
    2 Starflash Medium Lasers
    1 Conan DT-10 LRM Launcher
Manufacturer: Leopard Armor of Terra
Communications System: Trannel GL5
Targeting and Tracking System: Trannel OT73L

Overview:

Leopard Armor of Terra designed the Rhino in 2667 to have powerful weapons at long range. Other considerations were plainly secondary, as any Rhino crewman will agree. Crew comfort is nonexistent, and the ammunition storage area is ill-protected. The Rhino is also among the slowest military vehicles ever produced.

Capabilities:

When it appeared in 2669 to anchor defensive lines, the Rhino impressed commanders with its weaponry and thick slab armor. Though uncomfortable, the Rhino offers one of the most complete weapon packages available. The Rhino relies mostly on missiles, but it also carries lasers in case it runs out of missiles. The Rhino's primary weapons are the twin Delta Dagger LRM-20 systems in the turret and the Conan DT-10 LRM in the hull. Two turret-mounted Starflash medium lasers complete the armament.

The LRM launchers provide heavy support for armored companies, with the effect of a miniature artillery barrage. Notably absent from the Rhino is a Cellular Ammunition Storage Equipment system for the missile reloads.

Type: **Rhino**

Equipment		Mass
Internal Structure:		8
Engine:	Pitban 240	17.25
Type:	Fusion	
Cruise Speed:	3	
Flank Speed:	5	
Heat Sinks:	10	0
Control Equipment:		4
Lift Equipment:		0
Power Amplifier		0
Turret:		2.2
Armor Factor:	272	17

	Armor Value
Front	64
Left Side	54
Right Side	54
Rear	40
Turret	60

Weapons and Ammo:	Location	
LRM20	Turret	10
LRM20	Turret	10
AMMO LRM 20 (18)	Body	3
Medium Laser	Turret	1
Medium Laser	Turret	1
LRM10	Hull	5
AMMO LRM 10 (12)	Body	1

Mass: 95 tons
Movement Type: Tracked
Power Plant: Pitban 285
Cruising Speed: 32 kph
Flank Speed: 49 kph
Armor: AmberStar Weave
Armament:
2 Holly-20 Long Range Missile Racks
1 Donal Technologies Particle Cannon
2 Krieger Medium Lasers
1 Holly-4 Short Range Missile Rack
1 SkyLight Model 5 Flamer
1 Krieger Small Laser
Manufacturer: Pandora 'Mech Works Inc.
Communications System: COMTEC 400E
Targeting and Tracking System: GroundTracker EE-4

Overview:

In many respects, the Puma resembles designs that predate the 'Mech. It is slow, bulky, and armed with a variety of weapons. It poses a threat to small BattleMechs, but its size and immobility limit its usefulness. The modifications in the latest model of the Puma, the PMA 005 BP, show some promise for giving this vehicle greater flexibility.

The Puma has had a poor image from the start because it was designed by a company that had previously only built BattleMechs. The first model, produced in 2650, was the PMA 001, which had some

success. Its promise offset its problems, and so Pandora pushed forward. The main weakness was that the environmental controls did not account for the modern battlefield, and many crews perished because of gas or radiation. The temperature inside the PMA 001 issue exceeded 120 degrees during combat, hindering the performance of the crew and machinery.

Later models of the Puma sought to correct those early difficulties but created new problems. The modifications in the 002 made the quarters survivable, but affected the LRM ammunition-feed system to the point where it jammed frequently. Engineers from Holly Inc. corrected the feed, only to have Pandora's engineers alter the coolant coils for the laser systems. By the time of the 005 model, engineers had created a battle-worthy Puma, but it suffered from its bad reputation with the press and with tank crews.

Capabilities:

The Puma's main strength is its firepower from a variety of weapons. The Donal PPC mounted in the turret delivers the most damage, but the Puma also carries long- and short-range missiles, laser systems, and even a rear-mounted flamer. The weapons mix allows the Puma to perform well in a variety of combat situations.

The Puma PMA-005 BP has long-range striking power with the twin-mounted Holly Racks, mounted on the sides of the tank in hinged armored doors that open forward. The racks pivot 60 degrees forward, allowing the missiles to fire directly forward or angle to the sides, an unusual arrangement even in the vast arsenal of the Star League. Veteran infantry have learned not to stand next to the Puma's missile doors.

The Puma has a number of emergency hatches for the crew, which has improved its reputation somewhat. The most innovative one is in the floor of the tank. Activating the hatch sets off a small charge, blasting a foxhole or escape trench for those trying to leave the tank. This is another unique feature of the Puma.

The weakest part of any tank is usually the rear. This is true of the Puma, but the PMA 005 BP protects itself with a Skylight Model 5 flamer and a Krieger small laser. These light armaments are little use against 'Mechs, but they are effective in discouraging infantry who circle behind the Puma. The turret gunnery officer controls both of these systems, which means that the tank has great difficulty firing forward and backward at the same time.

Military experts find fault with the Puma's armor configuration on several counts. They consider the edges of the tank too sharp and the angle of the armor too steep to deflect shots.

Maintenance on the Puma initially was a nightmare for the technical services. Due to the variety of systems and subcontractors on the Puma, spare parts are a problem.

Type: **Puma**

Equipment		Mass
Internal Structure:		9.5
Engine:	Pitban 285	24.75
Type:	Fusion	
Cruise Speed:	3	
Flank Speed:	5	
Heat Sinks:	16	
		4.75
Lift Equipment:		0
Power Amplifier		0
Turret:		0.7
Armor Factor:	208	13

	Armor Value
Front	52
Left Side	40
Right Side	40
Rear	25
Turret	51

Weapons and Ammo:	Location	
LRM20	Right	10
LRM20	Left	10
AMMO LRM 20 (12)	Body	2
PPC	Turret	7
Medium Laser	Front	1
Medium Laser	Front	1
SRM 4	Front	2
AMMO SRM 4 (25)	Body	1
Flamer	Rear	1
Small Laser	Rear	0.5

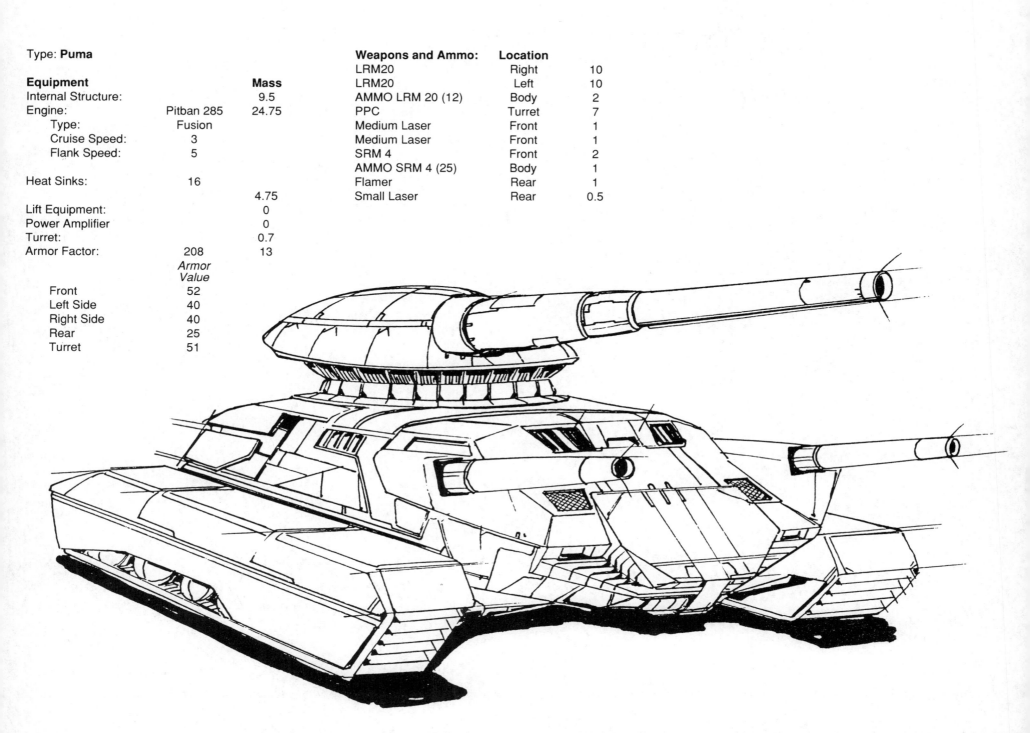

WARSHIPS

5

The warships of the Star League were massive, armed battlecruisers able to maneuver in space for combat purposes as well as jump from star to star carrying DropShips. The Star League Navy depended on its fearsome warships to enforce its authority over the thousands of planets owing it allegiance across the vastness of space. These giant ships were used to escort transports carrying the familiar DropShips or alone to threaten an unruly world's orbiting assets, such as Zero-G industries or space stations.

Because their major targets were other ships or such orbiting assets, Star League JumpShips differed from those of the present era. Though current-day JumpShips are considered huge, they would have seemed no more than small transports in the heyday of the League.

Star League warships were constructed with turrets and missile launchers fore and aft, separated by bridge towers and antenna, with secondary weapons and fighter bays, if any, along the central shaft.

The warship's weaponry was designed to take on other warships and was not bound by the space restrictions facing DropShips. Certain weapons resemble those known today, but with features greatly extending range and effectiveness, while others have gone the way of other lostech. Because of the size of these weapons, they could not target anything smaller than a DropShip.

With the fall of the Star League and the start of centuries of warfare known as the Succession Wars, much advanced technology and industrial capacity has been destroyed as the House Lords of the Inner Sphere battle for dominance. Current JumpShip construction capabilities have been reduced to a minute fraction that can barely keep up with annual losses of JumpShips. Most existing JumpShips are centuries old, with only about 12 per year produced among all the states of the Inner Sphere. Though new ships are being built, the technology underlying the Kearny-Fuchida jump drive has been lost to the depredations of war. Therefore, new JumpShip types cannot be created, nor have the Successor States been able to recreate the superior capabilities of the Star League-era models.

The Lyran Commonwealth's *LCS Invincible* was possibly the last capital warship seen in the Inner Sphere. In 2853, the Draconis Combine attempted yet another attack on the 'Mech factories of Hesperus II, to which the desperate Lyrans responded by calling in the *LCS Invincible*, which was considered little more than a museum piece at the time. In a dramatic show of power, the powerful warship broke the Kurita blockade of the Hesperus II, then bombarded half the Combine's men, fighters, and DropShips into oblivion. Also destroyed in this hard-fought battle were the last of the Kurita warships, dwarfs in comparison to the *Invincible*. Ironically, the *Invincible* vanished forever when its K-F drive failed in mid-jump on its way back to Tharkad.

NAVAL AUTOCANNON

Though the autocannon common in the Inner Sphere today formed the secondary armament of Star League warships, another class of autocannon often gave warships their offensive punch. Known as Naval Autocannon, or NAC, these autocannon were quite large and used huge neo-cordite (nitroglycerine and other explosives in a stabilizing jelly) charges to propel the projectiles much farther than common autocannon.

These cannon were mounted in turrets, and in smaller ships, in a single gun turret. Larger ships used double, triple, and even quadruple turrets with curved, sloping armor. Occasionally, ships might fix one of the NAC inside the ship, with its muzzle pointing out the side, rather than in a turret.

Regular autocannon and smaller naval autocannon often had their own turrets mounted on the sides of the ships. These guns might be used to protect the AeroSpace Fighter bays during launch and landing.

All turrets were designed to give the weapon the maximum range of elevation needed in space combat.

	NAVAL AUTOCANNON*					
	Short	**Medium**	**Long**	**Tons**	**Tons/Shot**	**Damage**
NAC/10	1 – 8	9 – 16	17 – 24	2,000	.2	100
NAC/20	1 – 8	9 – 16	17 – 24	2,500	.4	200
NAC/25	1 – 7	8 – 14	15 – 21	3,000	.6	250
NAC/30	1 – 7	8 – 14	15 – 21	3,500	.8	300
NAC/35	1 – 6	7 – 12	13 – 18	4,000	1.	350
NAC/40	1 – 5	6 – 10	11 – 15	4,500	1.2	400

* May only be used against DropShip size targets or larger

MISSILES

Not limited by the cramped quarters inside Drop-Ships, fighters, and 'Mechs, missiles came into their own in the warships of the Star League Navy. There were three basic classes. The largest and heaviest was the Killer Whale. Slightly smaller was the White Shark missile, which was harder for the enemy to shoot down. The wiliest missile was the Barracuda, which traded its offensive punch for a sophisticated computer program that almost guaranteed its success.

LASERS AND PPCS

Lasers used on warships were much larger and worked to a greater range than current models.

Because Star League lasers had superior fiber technology and emitter crystals, these lasers did not have to be mounted on long, gun-like mechanisms. On warships, lasers were nothing more than slits on turrets or on the sides of ships.

PPCs need a gun-like projection system and often used a turret similar to those for naval autocannon.

LITHIUM-FUSION BATTERIES

The Lithium-Fusion Battery was an exceptional bit of Star League technology that opened up new tactics and altered the strategy of deployment. Essentially a storage cell for massive amounts of solar energy, the Lithium-Fusion Battery allowed a ship to save the power needed to activate its Kearny-Fuchida drive. A ship on station could collect the energy with its sail to recharge its drive coils, then keep collecting energy for its L-F Battery. A ship could also transfer power from a spacestation or recharging facility directly into its L-F Battery, thereby eliminating the need to wait for its drive coils to recharge.

A warship equipped with Lithium-Fusion Batteries could jump into a system, find itself in an ambush, and immediately jump back to a friendly system. The Star League also equipped many spacestations with Lithium-Fusion Batteries to give ships a quick infusion of energy to continue their journeys. Thus, in an emergency, a ship could jump into a system, siphon the energy from the station's cells, and jump to another system with another spacestation. Star League ships could cover great distances in a short time by using this method.

The single drawback to the L-F Battery is its enormous cost. Installing this device on a warship could almost double its cost, and so few ships carried the L-F. Many spacestations did have this equipment, but many more did not. Few spacestations outside the Terran Hegemony carried the Lithium-Fusion because of the Hegemony's fear of losing this technological advantage.

This device put an end to the use of the jump point-ambush as a system defense. The Star League Navy revolutionized tactics in the Brisbane system of the Taurian Concordat. A destroyer, the *Monmouth*, arrived at the zenith jump point to face twelve rebel ships. No doubt to their great surprise, the *Monmouth* immediately jumped back to the Rollis system. The *Monmouth*'s captain briefed the rest of the flotilla, which proceeded to jump to Brisbane's nadir jump point and began to burn toward the planet, catching the rebel ships flat-thrustered.

MISSILES

	Damage	Short	Medium	Long	Tons
Killer Whale	40	1 – 10	11 – 20	21 – 30	50
White Shark	30	1 – 15	16 – 25	26 – 39	40
Barracuda	20	1 – 20	21 – 26	27 – 30	30

NAVAL LASERS*

	Damage	Short	Medium	Long	Tons
Naval Laser 35	35	1 – 7	8 – 14	15 – 21	700
Naval Laser 45	45	1 – 9	10 – 18	19 – 27	900
Naval Laser 55	55	1 – 10	11 – 20	21 – 30	1,100

PPCS*

	Min	Damage	Short	Medium	Long	Tons
Light NPPC	4	70	1 – 8	9 – 16	17 – 24	1,400
Med. NPPC	5	90	1 – 10	11 – 20	21 – 30	1,800
Heavy NPPC	6	150	1 – 10	11 – 20	21 – 30	3,000

* May only be used against DropShip size targets

Mass: 6,100 tons
Crew: 20
K-F Drive System: Delano 2070
Interplanetary Engines: 2 Quadrant Turbo
Thrusters
Hull: Ferron 240
    Length: 129 meters
    Sail Span: 86 meters (detachable)
    DropShip Capacity: None
    AeroSpace Fighter Capacity: None
    Small Craft Complement: None
Armor: Mitchell 6HY
Armament:
    1 HellStar Light Particle Projection Cannon
    2 Selitex-25 Series Large Lasers
    1 Luxor-20 Series Autocannon
Manufacturer: Bowie Industries
Communications System: Farralex BT
Targeting and Tracking System: Tokina 9000R

Overview:

The Terran Hegemony, surrounded as it is by five often-belligerent neighbors, has an ongoing interest in its neighbors' affairs. Thus, the Hegemony Armed Forces places a high priority on the creation of surveillance vessels. The HAF is willing to invest considerably in vessels able to gather information in foreign star systems and escape without the world's defenders being the wiser. The Hegemony's sophisticated technology has created a whole family of surveillance vessels whose abilities far surpass anything the other realms have been able to produce. The *Bug-Eye* is one of the most successful of these vessels.

In 2524, when it became obvious that the aging *Nightwing* and *Tracker* surveillance vessels were too outmoded for refitting with new electronics, the Hegemony put out a call for a new ship class. Twelve shipyards submitted design proposals, with Bowie Industries of Wasat winning the contract. Construction of the first *Bug-Eye* vessel was completed easily, despite the ship's small size for the amount of equipment it was to carry. After long and distinguished service with the HAF, the first *Bug-Eye* surveillance vessel entered service with the Star League Navy in 2620. It was commissioned the *SLS Mata Hari*.

Capabilities:

The *Bug-Eye*'s outward appearance is intended to mimic the *Buccaneer*, *Sylvester*, and other commonly sighted classes of merchant vessels, but beneath its drab exterior are some of the most sophisticated sensing devices and computers developed to date. Probes, dishes, even the hull of the vessel can pick up communications from either ships or planetary surfaces.

This equipment is so sensitive that enemy vessel captains have been known to forbid their bridge personnel to speak, for fear that a *Bug-Eye* would overhear. This caution may have a solid basis, as late-model *Bug-Eyes* are reported able to hack into some vessels' computer systems and listen in on a ship's interior communications.

The famed Tokina Imaging Company of Terra has provided a collection of optical and electronic equipment that the *Bug-Eye* uses to collect such detailed information that crew members can read material held by a person thousands of kilometers below.

Electronics and configuration give the ship its ability to escape detection. When stimulated by low-level electricity, special materials used in both the hull and paint activate radar-absorbing properties that make the ship disappear from an enemy's screens. The ship also has the ability to mimic a wide variety of merchant-vessel call signs, making it that much more difficult to identify.

If detected and forced to run, the *Bug-Eye*'s two massive engines have far greater thrust than any civilian engines of comparable class, giving the ship deceptive speed and agility. Its jump drive, one of the most compact in any ship, requires very little power, dispensing with the typical large sail for a smaller, internally stored sail to absorb the needed energy.

As the Star League has no qualms about spying on either friend or foe, the SLDF uses *Bug-Eye* surveillance vessels widely. People all over the Star League assume that a *Bug-Eye* will be paying them a visit at least once a year, if not more frequently. Many find this idea offensive, while others find comfort in the League's diligence.

Type: **Bug-Eye**
Class: Surveillance
Structural Integrity: 20
K-F Drive Integrity: 2
Energy Collector Sail Integrity: 3
Docking Hard Points: None
Small Craft Cubicles: None
Small Craft Bay Doors: None
Grav Deck: None
Engine: Quadrant Turbo Thruster
    Thrust: 5
    Overthrust: 8
    Fuel (3 Thrust Points/ton): 320
    Consumption: 2.82 tons/burn-day
Armor Factor (16 points/ton): 1,520
    Nose: 304
    Right Side: 310
    Left Side: 310
    Fuselage: 400
    Engine: 196

Weapons	Location
Light PPC	Nose
Large Laser	Right Side
Large Laser	Left Side
AC/20	Rear

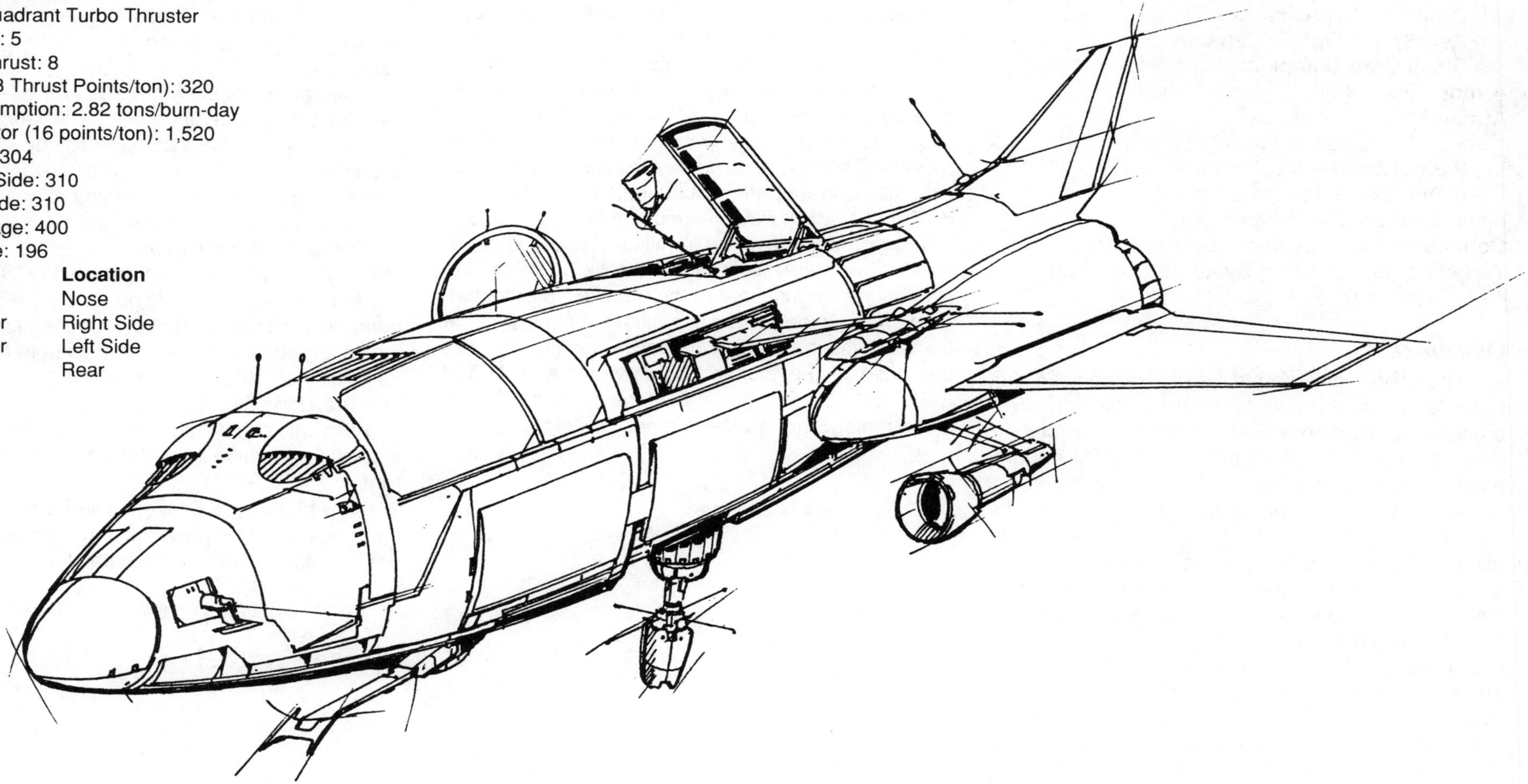

VINCENT

Mass: 412,000 tons
Crew: 113
K-F Drive System: KF Mark III-c
Interplanetary Engines: 2 Howser 2G2 "Hotfires"
Hull: Templar X-Plate
    Length: 402 meters
    Sail Span: 1005 meters (detachable)
    DropShip Capacity: None
    AeroSpace Fighter Capacity: 6
    Small Craft Complement: 4
Armor: Delhi 9800
Armament:
    4 Luxor-10 Series Naval Autocannon
    2 Barracuda Missile Tubes
    8 Thunderbolt Large Lasers.
Manufacturer: Delhi Warships
Communications System: Belden 405M
Targeting and Tracking System: Ulsop Eagle-
    Eye 12

Overview:

The Hegemony Armed Forces recognized the need for a small, powerful craft to patrol the approaches to Hegemony worlds. Being surrounded by Inner Sphere realms, the admirals of the HAF sought a patrol vessel that could delay any intruders.

For years, the Terran Hegemony had to make do with a variety of corvette designs that were poor compromises between detection capabilities and combat-worthiness. To cover the weaknesses, the HAF mixed corvettes of different types into four-ship squadrons. Thus, two *Bonaventure* Class ships, which had excellent surveillance capabilities but poor armament, patrolled with two of the *Vigilant* Class, which was well-armed but limited in its detection-capability. The Hegemony also relied heavily on remote surveillance satellites scattered throughout its star systems.

When the Capellan army invaded Terra Firma in 2409 with a large fleet and still caught the HAF off-guard, it pointed up the Terran Hegemony's continued vulnerability. After eventually recapturing Terra Firma, the Hegemony Armed Forces used a portion of the Liao reparations to commission a new corvette. The specifications for a new design called for detection-capability at twice the distance of previous corvettes, enough firepower to threaten any intruder, and the flexibility to incorporate future advances.

Delhi Ships, a small manufacturer of military transport vessels that later became Delhi Warships, submitted a design that would became the *Vincent* corvette. Though based outside the Hegemony, Delhi won the contract partly because its headquarters is on Capella, and it would take payment in the flood of L-Bills pouring into Terra in military reparations. To handle the huge contract and to keep secret the Hegemony technology being installed on the *Vincent,* Delhi Ships agreed to build a new facility in the Carver System. Delhi produced a design that was produced in the thousands, served the HAF and SLDF for more than three centuries, and built Delhi into a major Star League defense contractor.

Capabilities:

What set the *Vincent* apart from previous Hegemony corvettes was its size, almost twice that of previous designs, and the use of what the designers called "smart modularity."

Smart modularity was Delhi Ships' attempt to confer with other contractors to standardize ship fittings and systems. These pioneers in cooperation produced many components that are still used on new ships.

Though many crewmen found the large size of the *Vincent* corvette unnerving, that very feature is a key to the ship's longevity. The roomy *Vincent* has accommodated all technological advances. At one time or another, engineers have replaced the ship's engines, computers, and weapons.

The statistics provided here are for the *Vincent* Mark XXXIX, the most common model . The heart of the Mark XXXIX is its Ulsop AI Surveillance Computer, which is so efficient at gathering and interpreting data gathered by the ship's sensors that it nearly doubled the detection range of the Mark XXXVIII.

The ship's four naval autocannon, eight lasers, and two missile systems give it credible firepower, especially because corvettes usually fight as squadrons.

The Mark XXXIX carries two Howser 2G2 "Hotfire" engines. Their powerful thrust gives the *Vincent* great swiftness and maneuverability.

Type: **Vincent**
Class: Corvette
Structural Integrity : 40
K-F Drive Integrity: 10
Energy Collector Sail Integrity: 3
Docking Hard Points: None
Small Craft Cubicles: 10
Small Craft Bay Doors: 2
Grav Deck: 1
Engine: Howser 2G2 "Hotfire"
   Thrust: 4
   Overthrust: 6
   Fuel (1 Thrust Point/2 tons): 1,000
   Consumption: 39.52 tons/burn-day

Armor Factor (8 points/ton): 848
  Command Section
    Nose: 80
    Right Side: 110
    Left Side: 110
  Middle Section
    Right Side: 124
    Left Side: 124
  Engine Section
    Right Side: 110
    Left Side: 110
    Aft (Engine) 80

Weapons:
  Command Section (Nose Firing Arc)
    Nose:
      2 Barracuda Missiles
    Right Side:
      2 Large Laser
      1 NAC/10
    Left Side:
      2 Large Lasers
      1 NAC/10
  Middle Section
    Right Side:
      2 Large Lasers
      1 NAC/10
    Left Side:
      2 Large Lasers
      1 NAC/10
  Engine Section: None

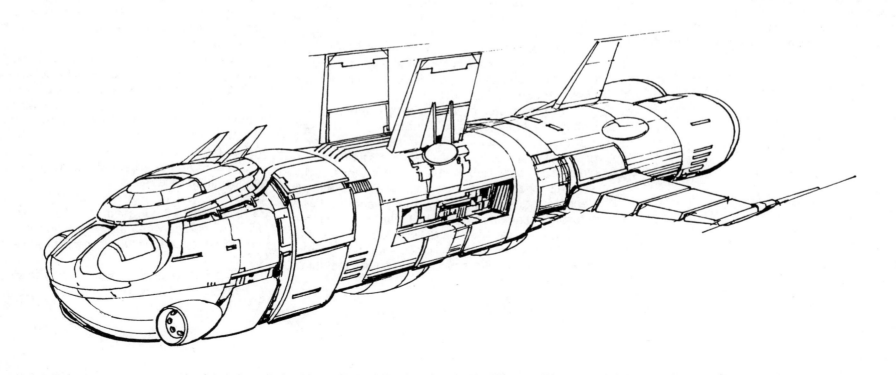

Mass: 612,000 tons
Crew: 208
K-F Drive System: KF Tri-Mark V
Interplanetary Engines: 3 InterSystem Class VIIs
Hull: FerroMite 90R
    Length: 615 meters
    Sail Span: 1,120 meters
    DropShip Capacity: None
    AeroSpace Fighter Capacity: 6
    Small Craft Complement: 4
Armor: MVT CL200
Armament:
    12 Whirlwind-20 Series Naval Autocannon
    3 Barracuda Missile Tubes (two forward, one aft)
    8 Rand-10 Medium Naval Particle Projection
      Cannon
    8 Magna-35 Naval Lasers
Manufacturer: Mitchell Vehicles
Communications System: Marcon DIY
Targeting and Tracking System: Diamond XR3

Overview:

There have been two classes of destroyers to bear the *Essex* name, the first seeing service in the Hegemony Navy during the 25th and 26th centuries. It was designed for sentinel duty in the space around important worlds as a command ship for squadrons of corvettes. The class performed well until 2645, when the new *Naga* Class began to replace the *Essex* destroyers.

In 2707, the Star League Defense Forces called for a new destroyer to supplant the *Naga*. Disenchanted with the slow *Baron* and *Carson* Classes, the Star League admirals wanted a quicker destroyer that could also make sustained voyages far from support.

Capabilities:

The *SLS Essex* slipped its moorings from the Mitchell Vehicles shipyards above Graham IV in late 2711. Because its designers had wished to emphasize the vessel's swiftness and reliability, they had given it three compact and dependable InterSystem Class VII engines, built by the Saro company of Keid, which produce great thrust.

The computer system is the Diamond Green Combat Computer, manufactured by the Nirasaki Computers Collective. Though not the most powerful or versatile computer available, it is one of the simplest and most reliable, qualities that Star League admirals prized. Beginning in the 2740s, Mitchell Vehicles started equipping the destroyers with Nirasaki's Diamond Plum, which can manage more tasks but requires special training. Both systems can control many remote surveillance satellites, orchestrate nearby corvette squadrons, and fire the ship's weapons.

The *Essex*'s main weapons are its twelve autocannon, manufactured by Karon Naval Armaments of Terra and mounted in four turrets. The Whirlwind-20 Series has been used for 100 years and is unmatched for reliability.

The *Essex* carries three missile tubes capable of firing Barracuda missiles, the smallest and smartest of the three standard missile types used by the Star League Navy.

One of the main flaws of the *Essex* is its ammunition bays, which are too lightly armored to protect the missiles and shells adequately. This drawback became evident with the destruction of two *Essex* destroyers in action against Periphery forces in the 2730s. Mitchell Vehicles added armor to the 300 *Essex* destroyers in service, but it lacks the structural strength of armor incorporated into the frame.

An *Essex* can carry six AeroSpace Fighters in a bay amidships that has entrances to the port and starboard.

[EDITOR'S NOTE: One of the most famous *Essex* Class destroyers was the *SLS Gettysburg*, launched in 2722. Under Major Alina Carrows, the *Gettysburg* served in the Periphery, overseeing the flow of ships in and out of the New Vandenberg star system, where the ship defeated an ancient *Dart* Class cruiser crewed by fanatical Periphery separatists.

In 2757, Major Evgeny Baratynsky, a decorated nephew of General Aleksandr Kerensky, took command of the *Gettysburg* from Major Val Mhong. Major Baratynsky and the crew of the ship showed great skill and courage when they were isolated from the rest of the Star League fleet in the Taurian Concordat region.

The *SLS Gettysburg* was destroyed by Caspar drone warships above Terra in 2777.]

Type: Essex
Class: Destroyer
Structural Integrity 60
K-F Drive Integrity: 15
Energy Collector Sail Integrity: 4
Docking Hard Points: 0
Small Craft Cubicles: 10
Small Craft Bay Doors: 2
Grav Deck: 1
Engine: InterSystem VII
   Thrust: 3
   Overthrust: 5
   Fuel (1 Thrust Point/2 tons): 600
   Consumption: 39.52 tons/burn-day
Armor Factor (6 points/ton): 1,830
   Command Section (Nose Firing Arc)
     Nose: 225
     Right Side: 225
     Left Side: 225
   Middle Section
     Right Side: 250
     Left Side: 250
   Engine Section
     Right Side: 225
     Left Side: 225
     Aft (Engine) 205

Weapons:
   Command Section (Nose Firing Arc)
     Nose:
       2 NAC/20s
     Right Side:
       3 NAC/20s
       1 Barracuda Missile
     Left Side:
       3 NAC/20s
       1 Barracuda Missile
   Middle Section
     Right Side:
       2 Medium Naval PPCs
       2 NL/35s
     Left Side:
       2 Medium Naval PPCs
       2 NL/35s

Engine Section
   Right Side:
     2 Medium Naval PPCs
     2 NL/35s
   Left Side:
     2 Medium Naval PPCs
     2 NL/35s
   Engine:
     4 NAC/20s
     1 Barracuda Missile

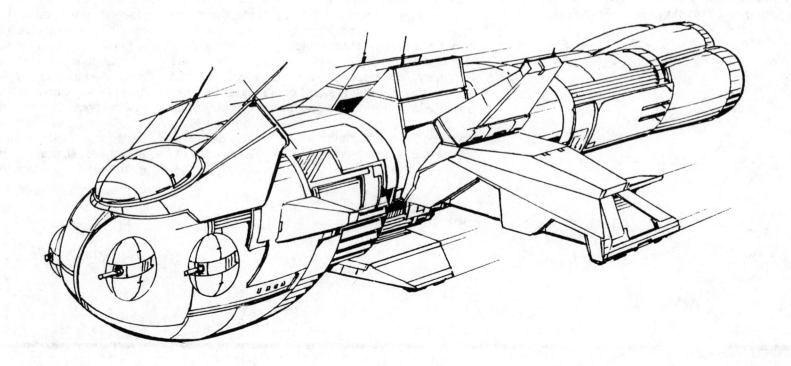

Mass: 678,000 tons
Crew: 154
K-F Drive System: KF King III
Interplanetary Engines: 4 Rolls LeFay
Hull: AlumaShield MX
    Length: 653 meters
    Sail Span: 1,100 meters
    DropShip Capacity: none
    AeroSpace Fighter Capacity: 6
    Small Craft Complement: 4
Armor: Boeing D-Span
Armament:
    12 Hellion-55 Series Naval Lasers
    2 White Shark Missile Tubes
    5 Barracuda Missile Tubes
    16 Luxor-10 Naval Autocannon
    4 Maxell-45 Series Naval Lasers
Manufacturer: Boeing Interstellar
Communications System: ViaComm 248
Targeting and Tracking: Delta Trac-VII

Overview:

This class of heavily armed and armored destroyers was named for an admiral who was one of the Hegemony Navy's harshest critics. Rear Admiral Adelaide Lola, one of the first commanders of Warship Sub-Command, was the conscience of the Hegemony Navy with her unrelenting demands that her sailors meet standards of moral and ethical excellence as well as military skill.

She died in 2332, and a destroyer class bearing her name was launched in 2345. The first *Lola* Class of destroyers served for 760 years in the HAF as an escort and picket ship. In 2622, Blue Nose Clipperships gave the name Lola to a design undergoing tests, but faults in the ship and budget constraints aborted the expected contract, leaving the *Lola II* as an orphan in navy service until the turn of the century.

Years after the *Lola II* entered service, reports about the increasing size and sophistication of Periphery raiders prompted the Quartermaster Command to seek a new vessel design. The specifications called for a destroyer that would be easy and inexpensive to build, strong enough for escort duties in the Periphery, and dependable enough for extended picket duty in the star systems of the Terran Hegemony. In 2660, after looking over the designs submitted by Hegemony shipbuilders, the Star League Navy awarded the contract for the *Lola III* class destroyer escort to Boeing Interstellar.

Capabilities:

The most obvious feature of the *Lola* is its impressive array of armaments. Four turrets hold twelve huge naval lasers of great power and the widest possible arcs of fire.

The other main armament consists of a mix of White Shark and Barracuda missile launchers.

The *Lola*'s secondary armament is also stronger then that carried on other destroyers. The 16 autocannon and four lasers frame the two entrances to the destroyers' hangar deck, which can carry a maximum of six heavy AeroSpace Fighters.

To meet the navy's request for a destroyer that can withstand punishment, Boeing Interstellar consulted with several BattleMech manufacturers about the most effective use of armor on the ship's hull. The 'Mech makers recommended the use of what was called baffled deadspace, a cushion layer between the inner and outer hull to absorb the impact of a weapon hit. The concept improved the *Lola*'s protection, but the innovative armor added too much weight to the ship. To counter the problem, Boeing Interstellar used four Rolls Le Fay interplanetary drives, engines designed for larger vessels. Using these engines in a destroyer left little room for anything else, making tight quarters throughout the *Lola*.

Even these engines did not make the *Lola* swift, but it can at least maneuver around transports. As an escort vessel, the *Lola* has no equal. A single *Lola* guarding a convoy is sufficient deterrent to keep most pirates at bay.

Type: **Lola**
Class: Destroyer
Structural Integrity: 50
K-F Drive Integrity: 20
Energy Collector Sail Integrity: 5
Docking Hard Points: None
Small Craft Cubicles: 10
Small Craft Bay Doors: 2
Grav Deck: None
Engine: Rolls LeFay
    Thrust: 4
    Overthrust: 6
    Fuel (1 Thrust Point/2 tons): 600
    Consumption: 39.52 tons/burn-day
Armor Factor (8 points/ton): 2,600
    Command Section
        Nose: 300
        Right Side: 300
        Left Side: 300
    Middle Section
        Right Side: 400
        Left Side: 400
    Engine Section
        Right Side: 300
        Left Side: 300
        Aft (Engine): 300

Weapons:
    Command Section (Nose Firing Arc)
        Nose:
            2 NL/55s
        Right Side:
            3 NL/55s
            1 White Shark Missile
        Left Side:
            3 NL/55s
            1 White Shark Missile

    Middle Section
        Right Side:
            4 NAC/10s
            1 NL/45
            2 Barracuda Missiles
        Left Side:
            4 NAC/10s
            1 NL/45
            2 Barracuda Missiles

Engine Section
    Right Side:
        4 NAC/10s
        1 NL/45s
    Left Side:
        4 NAC/10s
        1 NL/45s
    Engine:
        4 NL/55s
        1 Barracuda Missile

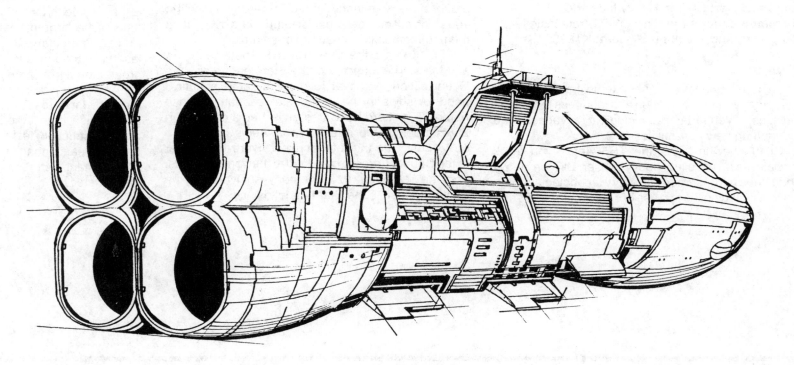

Mass: 745,000 tons
Crew: 180
K-F Drive System: KF Mark XIX
Interplanetary Engines: 2 Century 5000s
Hull: Templar Steel Plus
    Length: 725 meters
    Sail Span: 1,308 meters
    DropShip Capacity: 4
    AeroSpace Fighter Capacity: 18
    Small Craft Complement: 10
Armor: Grumman K5
Armament:
    18 Armstrong II 35-Series Naval Autocannon
    8 White Shark Missile Tubes
    24 Imperator-20 Naval Autocannon
    12 Randall-55 Naval Lasers
    4 Barracuda Missile Tubes
    4 Magna-45 Naval Lasers
Manufacturer: Di Tron Heavy Industries
Communications System: OMP Stratacaster
Targeting and Tracking System: KTI 389

Overview:

The *Aegis* heavy cruiser exemplifies the Terran Hegemony's love of tradition and fondness for proven designs, even after technological advances had opened up new possibilities.

Launched in 2372, the *THS Aegis* won quick acclaim as an excellent heavy cruiser. Di Tron Heavy Industries had incorporated every technological innovation, including the first use of detachable jump sails,

into the design of the *Aegis*. Detachable sails, which became common on warships by the end of the 24th century, allow the cruiser to protect the delicate mechanisms of the sail as it accelerates toward its target. Internal automated systems unfurl the sail in response to signals from the *Aegis* so that it begins collecting energy, storing it in several large batteries. This significantly reduces the time the cruiser needs to jump out of a star system.

With excellent firepower and good mobility, *Aegis* cruisers served the Hegemony navy for a century and a half, undergoing many refits to take advantage of new equipment. In 2531, the cruisers began to be phased out in favor of the new *Avatar* cruisers, which turned out to be a short-lived class. A few *Aegis* cruisers remained in the navy as training vessels.

Deborah Cameron, the cautious Director-General of the Terran Hegemony at the time, lowered the profile of the Hegemony Armed Forces by retiring the 106 ships but guarded against future wars by sending them to mothballs instead of scrapyards.

For 30 years, the ships orbited Sol between Terra and Mars. The founding of the Star League and the Reunification War that followed created a critical need for ships in the young Star League Defense Forces. First Lord Ian Cameron issued a directive in 2582 ordering the return of the *Aegis* cruisers to active duty. One-third of the cruisers were turned over to the Council Lords to be added to their private fleets, and the rest went to Hegemony shipyards to be refitted for use in the Star League Navy.

Di Tron transformed the relics into some of the most advanced warships of their time. The newer equipment was mostly smaller than the old, and there was enough room to add a few amenities, such as a Zero-G pool. One of the most important innovations was the Lithium Fusion Batteries, which allow *Aegis* cruisers to store enough power for several jumps.

The addition of the 70 *Aegis* cruisers gave the Star League Navy a major boost during its crucial formation. In battle, the revitalized *Aegis* cruisers performed as well as more modern ships. Though their hulls had weakened with age, the ships' firepower was such that only the largest warships dared approach. The *Aegis* remains an important part of the Star League Navy more than a century later.

Capabilities:

The main firepower of the *Aegis* is its 18 35-Series autocannon and eight White Shark missile tubes. The large-caliber cannon are housed in six turrets. Secondary armament consists of a mix of lasers, cannon, and missiles, mostly clustered around the fighter bays.

The interior of a refitted *Aegis* cruiser is roomy by modern standards. This allows the ship to carry more ammunition than other cruisers. Archaic materials and construction techniques make the hull of the cruiser weaker than on later ships. The materials used to manufacture the hull also leave the ship more easily detected.

Type: **Aegis**
Class: Heavy Cruiser
Sructural Integrity: 75
K-F Drive Integrity: 20
Energy Collector Sail Integrity: 5
Docking Hard Points: 4
Small Craft Cubicles: 28
Small Craft Bay Doors: 6
Grav Deck: 2
Engine: Century 5000
   Thrust: 2
   Overthrust: 3
   Fuel (1 Thrust Point/2 tons): 500
   Consumption: 39.52 tons/burn-day
Armor Factor (8 points/ton): 5,400
   Command Section
      Nose: 600
      Right Side: 700
      Left Side: 700
   Middle Section
      Right Side: 700
      Left Side: 700
   Engine Section
      Right Side: 700
      Left Side: 700
      Aft (Engine): 600

Weapons:
   Command Section (Nose Firing Arc)
      Nose:
         2 NAC/35s
      Right Side:
         2 NAC/35s
         3 White Shark Missiles
      Left Side:
         2 NAC/35s
         3 White Shark Missiles
   Middle Section
      Right Side:
         4 NAC/35s
         3 NL/55s
         1 Barracuda Missile
         6 NAC/20s

      Left Side:
         4 NAC/35s
         3 NL/55s
         1 Barracuda Missile
         6 NAC/20s
   Engine Section
      Right Side:
         6 NAC/20s
         3 NL/55s
         1 Barracuda Missile
      Left Side:
         6 NAC/20s
         3 NL/55s
         1 Barracuda Missile
      Engine
         4 NAC/35s
         2 White Shark Missiles
         4 NL/45s

Mass: 760,000 tons
Crew: 256
K-F Drive System: KF Mark XXV
Interplanetary Engines: 3 GM 8050 Starlifters
Hull: Endo Steel AN
　　Length: 703 meters
　　Sail Span: 1,207 meters
　　DropShip Capacity: 2
　　AeroSpace Fighter Capacity: 6
　　Small Craft Complement: 4
Armor: Blue Nose 440CL
Armament:
　　8 Oriente-30 Naval Autocannon
　　1 Killer Whale Missile Tube
　　2 White Shark Missile Tubes
　　8 Armstrong LN-10 Naval Autocannon
　　8 Magna-Large Lasers
Manufacturer: Dekirk Aerospace
Communications System: 5T Vargas
Targeting and Tracking System: Wolf 157

Overview:

Frigates have served in both the Hegemony Navy and then in the Star League Navy as heavily armed surveillance vessels. The first frigates of the Hegemony Navy were little more than cruisers, with sensors and imaging equipment replacing much of their weaponry. As the navy's sophistication increased, ships were designed to be swift, heavily armed, and capable of electronic espionage.

In 2536, the admirals of the Hegemony decided that the *Quixote* Class frigates had outlived their usefulness. Incidents between the frigates and the warships of the surrounding realms showed that the *Quixote* could be outmaneuvered by foreign ships of comparable size.

A year later, the architects of Dekirk Aerospace submitted a design that seemed so good that the HegemonyNavy accepted it without hesitation. Construction of the first *Congress* frigates met a serious obstacle in the form of a lawsuit filed by the Federated Suns against the shipyard and the Hegemony government. In the lawsuit, Challenge Systems, a shipbuilding firm from the Davion world of Galax, claimed that most of the *Congress* frigate was a Challenge design stolen by industrial spies employed by Dekirk.

The legal wrangling continued for three years until a compromise agreement was signed in 2540. In it, the Terran Hegemony and Dekirk Aerospace admitted no guilt but did include Challenge Systems as a partner in the construction of the new frigates. The navy of the Federated Suns also received a bargain price on some of the new frigates, with the more advanced Hegemony technology absent.

Capabilities:

Because of its dual mission as convoy escort and an information-gathering vessel in enemy territory, the *Congress* frigate had to be swift, well-armed, equipped with advanced snooping gear, and capable of extended voyages through adverse conditions. The *Congress* was such a good mix of all these qualities that the Terran Hegemony and then the Star League saw no need to replace the 200 ships of the class for many decades.

Much of their satisfaction came from the fact that the interior of the ships makes every square centimeter functional and accessible to all major systems for easy maintenance, a trademark of Dekirk ships. Another trait of the company was its attention to ergonomics, the science of comfortably fitting the machine to the man using it. The company went to great lengths to ensure that the crew would be as comfortable as possible.

The ship's main armament is its eight cannon in five turrets, one missile launcher capable of launching the huge Killer Whale missile, and two other missile launchers that fire White Shark missiles.

The *Congress* can carry two DropShips behind its sensor and observer towers. Most carry the *Pentagon* Class DropShips, which are little more than large gun platforms that detach from the frigate to fight. On special missions, the *Congress* can carry DropShips containing troops or 'Mechs.

If the *Congress* Class has a weakness, it is lack of fighter support. Fighter carriers, such as the *Vengeance* Class, often accompany *Congress* frigates.

Type: **Congress**
Class: Frigate
Structural Integrity: 75
K-F Drive Integrity: 20
Energy Collector Sail Integrity: 5
Docking Hard Points: 2
Small Craft: Cubicles: 10
Small Craft: Bay Doors: 2
Grav Deck: 1
Engine: GM 8050 Starlifter
   Thrust: 3
   Overthrust: 5
   Fuel (1 Thrust Point/2 tons): 1000
   Consumption: 39.52 tons/burn-day
Armor Factor (8 points/ton): 3,904
   Command Section
      Nose: 480
      Right Side: 480
      Left Side: 480R/L
   Middle Section
      Right Side: 500
      Left Side: 500
   Engine Section
      Right Side: 480
      Left Side: 480
      Aft (Engine) 504

Weapons
   Command Section (Nose Firing Arc)
     Nose:
        1 Killer Whale Missile Tube
     Right Side:
        2 NAC/30s
     Left Side:
        2 NAC/30s
   Middle Section
     Right Side:
        2 NAC/10s
        2 Large Lasers
        1 White Shark Missiles
     Left Side:
        2 NAC/10s
        2 Large Lasers
        1 White Shark Missiles

   Engine Section
     Right Side:
        2 NAC/10s
        2 Large Lasers
        1 NAC/30
     Left Side:
        2 NAC/10s
        2 Large Lasers
        1 NAC/30
     Engine:
        2 NAC/30s

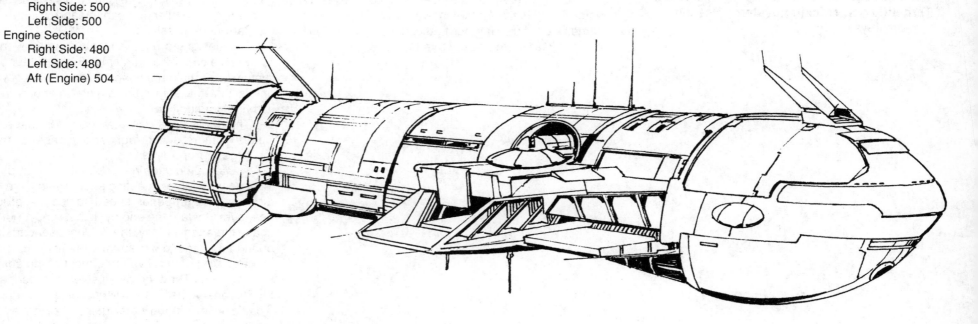

Mass: 802,000 tons
Crew: 208
K-F Drive System: KF King IX
Interplanetary Engines: 3 Carston Pegasus
Hull: ExoSteel C-180
    Length: 772 meters
    Sail Span: 1,433 meters
    DropShip Capacity: 4
    AeroSpace Fighter Capacity: 18
    Small Craft Complement: 10:
Armor: Grumman 900
Armament:
    18 Scarborough-30 Series Naval Autocannon
    8 White Shark Missile Tubes
    6 Barracuda Missile Tubes
    32 Imperator-20 Series Naval Autocannon
Manufacturer: Boeing Interstellar
Communications System: Needham AeroStar
Targeting and Tracking System: Needham
    OmniSystem IV

Overview:

When it became apparent that the *Cameron* battlecruisers were not living up to their design specifications, the Quartermaster Command decided to test a new design rather than pour trillions of Star League Dollars into redesigning and refitting existing *Cameron*s. The *Cameron*s remain in service, though in a much more limited role.

This time, the admirals of Warship Sub-Command bypassed the usual procedure of accepting design proposals from all the major shipyards, awarding the contract to Boeing Interstellar in late 2689. This award carried the proviso that the company would make several key modifications to a battlecruiser design it had submitted during the contract competition that led to the creation of the *Cameron*.

Boeing Interstellar produced an excellent design, named the *Black Lion* for former Director-General James McKenna's famous battlecruiser. Boeing built two per year for the next 31 years.

Capabilities:

The *Black Lion*'s three Carston Pegasus interplanetary engines generate almost twice as much thrust as those used on the *Cameron* Class. With less weight than the *Cameron*, the *Black Lion* became one of the quickest warships of its size. The engines' size and complexity, however, make the engineering decks a labyrinth of tight crawl-spaces and catwalks. Maintenance difficulties make engine breakdowns more frequent than normal for a modern ship.

The *Black Lion*'s second important improvement over the *Cameron* is increased armor protection. The most controversial aspect of the *Black Lion* is its choice of weapons. Instead of relying on energy weapons, the *Black Lion* mounts cannon and missiles as its primary weapons, four turrets carrying 30 Series autocannon and two turrets capable of firing White Shark missiles. The battlecruiser also carries four turrets of smaller autocannon and six tubes firing the Barracuda missiles.

The designers used only non-energy weapons so the ship could mount a smaller and lighter power system. The main drawback to this choice of weapons is that the ship must devote interior space to carrying ammunition.

The ship's flight deck can carry 18 heavy AeroSpace Fighters, and its four docking rings can handle the largest DropShips.

A *Black Lion* often heads a battle group protecting a convoy. When meeting enemy ships, the *Black Lion* uses its superior speed to lead a group of destroyers toward the enemy. If that is not enough to chase the enemy away, the battlecruiser can deliver enough damage to weaken the enemy's attack.

The *Black Lion*s live up to most of the admirals' expectations. They are as elusive as hoped, and in the Periphery, the battlecruisers can easily dominate a battle. In the hidden wars against the House militaries, however, *Black Lion*s cannot cope with swarms of enemy fighters.

Type: **Black Lion**
Class: Battlecruiser
Structural Integrity:75
K-F Drive Integrity: 20
Energy Collector Sail Integrity: 5
Docking Hard Points: 4
Small Craft Cubicles: 28
Small Craft Bay Doors: 6
Grav Deck: 2
Engine: Carston Pegasus
    Thrust: 3
    Overthrust: 5
    Fuel (1 Thrust Point/2 tons): 500
    Consumption: 39.52 tons/burn-day
Armor Factor (10 points/ton): 9,270
    Command Section
        Nose: 1,035
        Right Side: 1,200
        Left Side: 1,200
    Middle Section
        Right Side: 1,200
        Left Side: 1,200
    Engine Section
        Right Side: 1,200
        Left Side: 1,200
        Aft (engine): 1,035

Weapons:
    Command Section (Nose Firing Arc)
        Nose:
            4 NAC/30s
        Right Side:
            4 White Shark Missiles
            1 Barracuda Missile
            4 NAC/30s
        Left Side:
            4 White Shark Missiles
            1 Barracuda Missile
            4 NAC/30s

Middle Section
    Right Side:
        8 NAC/20s
        1 Barracuda Missiles
    Left Side:
        8 NAC/20s
        1 Barracuda Missiles
Engine Section
    Right Side:
        8 NAC/20s
        1 Barracuda Missiles
    Left Side:
        8 NAC/20s
        1 Barracuda Missiles
    Engine:
        6 NAC/30s

Mass: 823,000 tons
Crew: 201
K-F Drive System: KF King LX
Interplanetary Engines: 2 Harlan B8-160s
Hull: 40X Templar
    Length: 803 meters
    Sail Span: 1,250 meters
    DropShip Capacity: 4
    AeroSpace Fighter Capacity: 18
    Small Craft Complement: 8
Armor: Bowman JK3
Armament:
    12 Imperator-20 Series Naval Autocannon
    2 Killer Whale Missile Tubes
    4 Barracuda Missile Tubes
    24 Sorenstein-45a Series Naval Lasers
    8 Ceres-N Particle Projection Cannons
Manufacturer: Blue Nose Clipperships
Communications System: KAT 701
Targeting and Tracking System: ASTROC 4-b

Overview:

After being forced to sit by for years while the unstable Lord Jonathan Cameron devoted most of the League's military budget to automated space defense systems, the SLDF regained control of its finances when Mother Jocasta Cameron assumed most of the First Lord's duties in 2734. While the League had been focusing on fortification of Hegemony worlds, the private armies and navies of the Star League Member States had been growing strong. In response, General Rebecca Fredasa issued the New Arms Order of 2735, declaring her intention of reasserting the SLDF's superiority with new ships and weapons. Among the new ships that sprang from this order was the *Sovetskii Soyuz* cruiser.

Naval architects at Blue Nose Clipperships envisioned the *Sovetskii Soyuz* as a vessel with fearsome fighting abilities capable of fleet missions or independent actions.

Capabilities:

The *Soyuz* packs so much punch that many officers consider it a battlecruiser rather than a heavy cruiser. Leading the impressive list of weapons are twelve autocannon, housed in four turrets. Complementing the cannon turrets are three missile launchers, one firing the huge Killer Whales and the other two firing the smaller and more agile Barracudas.

Adequate space for missile and cannon ammunition was a problem that the ship's designers solved with automation. Three sophisticated Hornblower computer systems monitor and direct the ammunition-feed systems. Created by the Nirasaki Computers Collective, the computers and machinery assumed the tasks of 80 sailors. This frees up considerable space for ammunition, as well as for the large fighter hangar that holds 18 fighters.

Though this saved space, the only way to keep the ship reasonably swift and still carry so many weapons was to armor the hull rather lightly. Many officers feared that the ships would be "One-Shot Wonders" that would crumple under enemy fire, but such has not been the case. Because of their excellent training, Star League ship commanders have a knack for using their ship's strengths and masking its weaknesses.

The *Soyuz* carries docking rings for four DropShips, but only medium and smaller ships can attach.

In use, the *Soyuz* vindicated its unusual design. The automation has performed well, though there have been instances when the computers had what the sailors referred to as "brain seizures," requiring manual override and precious minutes to fix. In combat, the weaponry and speed serve the 400 *Soyuz* Class cruisers well.

Type: **Sovetskii Soyuz**
Class: Heavy Cruiser
Structural Integrity: 80
K-F Drive Integrity: 25
Energy Collector Sail Integrity: 5
Docking Hard Points: 4
Small Craft Cubicles: 26
Small Craft Bay Doors: 6
Grav Deck: 2
Engine: Harlan B-8 160
   Thrust: 2
   Overthrust: 3
   Fuel (1 Thrust Point/ 2 tons): 700
   Consumption: 39.52 tons/burn-day
Armor Factor (6 points/ton): 44,564
   Command Section
      Nose: 464
      Right Side: 600
      Left Side: 600
   Middle Section
      Right Side: 600
      Left Side: 600
   Engine Section
      Right Side: 600
      Left Side: 600
      Aft (Engine): 400

Weapons:
   Command Section (Nose Firing Arc)
      Nose:
         2 Killer Whale Missiles
      Right Side:
         3 NL/45s
         1 Barracuda Missile
      Left Side:
         3 NL/45s
         1 Barracuda Missile
   Middle Section
      Right Side:
         3 NAC/20s
         2 Medium Naval PPCs
      Left Side:
         3 NAC/20s
         2 Medium Naval PPCs

Engine Section
   Right Side:
      3 NAC/20s
      2 Medium Naval PPCs
      1 Barracuda Missile
   Left Side:
      3 NAC/20s
      2 Medium Naval PPCs
      1 Barracuda Missile
   Engine: None

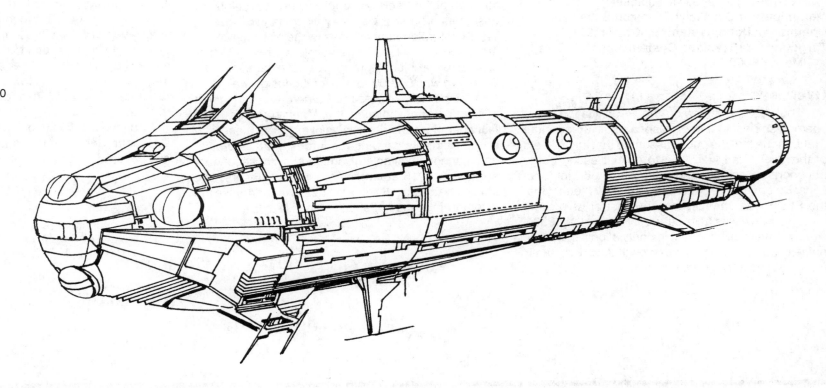

CAMERON

Mass: 859,000
Crew: 287
K-F Drive System: KF King VI-a
Interplanetary Engines: 2 Cassion Vassers
Hull: Creighton M-4
    Length: 839 meters
    Sail Span: 1,450 meters
    DropShip Capacity: 2
    AeroSpace Fighter Capacity: 16
    Small Craft Complement: 10
Armor: Ajax 7PK300
Armament:
    8 Maelstrom AR-10 Missile Launchers
    12 Super-Rand Heavy Naval Particle Projection
      Cannon
    16 Pontiac-25 Series Naval Autocannon
    10 Tronel-55 Series Naval Lasers
Manufacturer: Daussault-Shimmon Enterprises
Communications System: ViaComm1011
Targeting and Tracking System: Johnson Data
    Master 6000

Overview:

The decades following the Reunification Wars seemed so peaceful and prosperous all acrosss the Star League that the public assumed that the soldiers of the SLDF had very little to do but escort cargo transports or act as honor guard at important functions. So good were the times that many thought that the SLDF was unnecessary, at least at its present size. This view was at its strongest during the 2650s, when a small but influential minority of politicians and nobles lobbied to limit the growth and eventually freeze the military's budget.

The budget freeze forced the SLDF to be frugal, but there was a wide gap between the navy's battleships and its cruisers. The admirals needed a ship to assume command of the huge convoys going into and out of the Periphery. They wanted a ship with the firepower of a battleship and the mobility of a cruiser so it could keep up with the fast cargo DropShips being built at that time.

The small firm of Daussault-Shimmon Enterprises of New Earth beat out the other bidders for the contract in 2657. Instead of fulfilling its grand promises, the Cameron battlecruiser became the Star League Navy's biggest boondoggle.

Capabilities:

When launched in 2668, the Cameron obviously fell short of the sleek, powerful vessel promised by its designers. The ship was very slow. Its two Cassion Vasser interplanetary engines, while extremely powerful, could only match the acceleration of a battleship. The problem sprang from the fact that the Cameron was 50,000 tons over its design weight.

The good news was the Cameron's weaponry. It has four turrets housing the Maelstrom AR-10, a launcher that can fire missiles of any size, along with six other turrets carrying the largest particle projection cannon available. Combined with secondary armament of 16 autocannon, ten naval lasers, and the ability to carry 16 fighters, these weapons give the ship a tremendous offensive capability.

[Editor's Note: Though the admirals knew the Cameron was a flawed design, the prospect of public disapproval made them afraid to admit the mistake, and so they ordered 40 of the ships.

Modifications masked some of the many flaws, but hopes that the ship would turn out to be adequate were dashed by the fate of the SLS Saint Joan. Attached to the Twentieth Army in the Rim Worlds Republic, the Saint Joan escorted convoys carrying personnel and supplies for the SLDF. In November 2674, while escorting a convoy headed for Placidia, the ship encountered six privateer vessels, destroyer-size transports fitted with weapons and more powerful engines.

When the Saint Joan maneuvered to engage the attackers, it lost power. The captain switched to auxiliary power, only to find that the ship's batteries could not provide life support and fire the weapons simultaneously. Seeing that the battlecruiser was doing nothing to protect its ships, the privateers moved to investigate. After a few cautious attacks, they realized the vessel was helpless and so began to attack in earnest, destroying the Saint Joan in minutes.

An investigation later revealed that engineers at Daussault-Shimmon had known of the problem but had covered it up to save the contract.]

Type: **Cameron**
Class: Battlecruiser
Structural Integrity: 80
K-F Drive Integrity: 20
Energy Collector Sail Integrity: 5
Docking Hard Points: 2
Small Craft Cubicles: 16
Small Craft Bay Doors: 6
Grav Deck: 2
Engine: Cassion Vasser
    Thrust: 2
    Overthrust: 4
    Fuel (1 Thrust Point/2 tons): 500
    Consumption: 39.52 tons/burn-day
Armor Factor (8 points/ton): 7,016
    Command Section
      Nose: 816
      Right Side: 900
      Left Side: 900
    Middle Section
      Right Side: 900
      Left Side: 900
    Engine Section
      Right Side: 900
      Left Side: 900
      Aft (Engine): 800

Weapons:
    Command Section (Nose Firing Arc)
      Nose:
        2 Heavy Naval PPCs
      Right Side:
        2 AR-10s
        2 Heavy Naval PPCs
      Left Side:
        2 AR-10s
        2 Heavy Naval PPCs
    Middle Section
      Right Side:
        4 NAC/25s
        3 NL/55s
      Left Side:
        4 NAC/25s
        3 NL/55s

Engine Section
    Right Side:
      4 NAC/25s
      2 NL/55s
      2 AR10s
      2 Heavy Naval PPCs
    Left Side:
      4 NAC/25s
      2 NL/55s
      2 AR10s
      2 Heavy Naval PPCs
    Engine:
      2 Heavy Naval PPCs

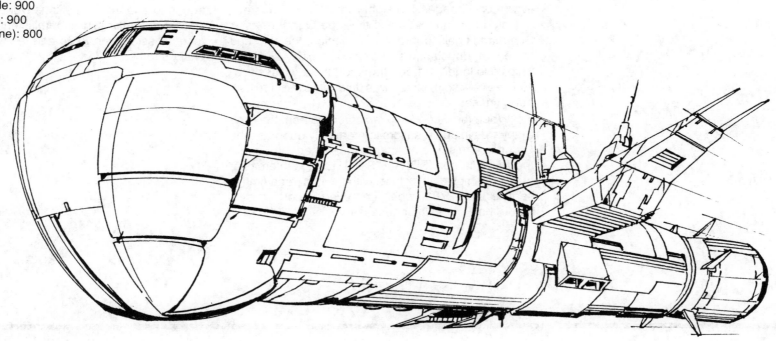

POTEMKIN

Mass: 1,508,000 tons
Crew: 226
K-F Drive System: KF Mark LC
Interplanetary Engines: 4 Chatham 7500s
Hull: Cortex DuoStress
    Length: 1508 meters
    Sail Span: 1,345 meters
    DropShip Capacity: 25 (Five per row)
    AeroSpace Fighter Capacity: none
    Small Craft Complement: 10
Armor: Grumman TR8
Armament:
    16 Maxell-45 Series Naval Lasers
    8 Barracuda Missile Tubes
    40 Fusigon-2a Medium Naval Particle Projection
      Cannon
Manufacturer: Riga Interstellar Shipyards
Communications System: TelStar HN
Targeting and Tracking System: KTI 600I

Overview:

The *Potemkin* cruiser is one of the oddest ships ever to see service. Its huge size and the fact that 25 DropShips hang from the cylindrical hull make this one of the most recognizable warships in the Star League. [EDITOR'S NOTE: This ship was twice the length of today's *Monolith* JumpShip.]

The Reunification War taught the SLDF that DropShips carrying troops were poorly equipped to defend themselves in space. The Quartermaster Command therefore called for a cruiser that could defend DropShips and that was also nimble enough to avoid enemy ships.

In 2601, Riga Interstellar Shipyards submitted the original design, which would carry ten DropShips and be about half the size of what the *Potemkin* eventually became. Though generally pleased with the design, the SLDF sent it back to Riga with suggested modifications. Riga Interstellar resubmitted an improved design, only to get it back yet again with even more changes. For eight years, the bureaucratic redesign continued. By the time the Quartermaster Command finally approved the design, the ship had more than doubled in size and could carry 25 Drop-Ships. No longer a troop transport by any classification, the new ship design was uniquely classified as a troop cruiser.

When the *SLS Potemkin* emerged from the Riga Shipyards in 2611, sailors immediately dubbed it the Corncob Cruiser, a nickname that lasted throughout the ship's career. [EDITOR'S NOTE: Riga Interstellar built 106 ships of this class, with the last remaining in service until 2781, when improved escort vessels made the *Potemkin* unnecessary.]

Capabilities:

The *Potemkin* carries 25 DropShips in five rows of five around the cruiser's cylindrical hull. The arrangement of the docking rings protects the DropShips but allows most of their weapons to fire.

The weapons on *Potemkin* cruisers are chosen for their effectiveness against AeroSpace Fighters. Among and around the DropShip rings are 20 turrets carrying medium PPCs. Five turrets carrying large lasers and eight Barracuda missile launchers are clustered around the nose and engines of the ship.

Though *Potemkin* cruisers perform well in battle, they are not without flaws. The enormous fuel requirements of 25 DropShips make it necessary for each *Potemkin* to travel with tankers, which themselves require escort.

[EDITOR'S NOTE: Launched in 2748, the *SLS Riga* was one of the last *Potemkin* cruisers to be built. Under Commodore Nicholas Schlesinger, the *Riga* saw considerable action in the Periphery, ferrying troops to and from rebellious worlds. The *Riga* was the last *Potemkin* to be commissioned, in 2781. It was recommissioned in 2784 and left with General Kerensky's forces.]

Type: **Potemkin**
Class: Troop Cruiser
Structural Integrity: 80
K-F Drive Integrity: 20
Energy Collector Sail Integrity: 5
Docking Hard Points: 25
Small Craft Cubicles: 10
Small Craft Bay Doors: 2
Grav Deck: 1
Engine: Chatham 7500
    Thrust: 2
    Overthrust: 3
    Fuel (1 Thrust Point/2 tons): 5,000
    Consumption: 39.52 tons/burn-day
Armor Factor (8 points/ton): 10,928
    Command Section
        Nose: 1,228
        Right Side: 1,450
        Left Side: 1,450
    Center Section
        Right Side: 1,450
        Left Side: 1,450
    Engine Section
        Right Side: 1,450
        Left Side: 1,450
        Aft (Engine): 1,000

Weapons:
    Command Section (Nose Firing Arc)
        Nose:
            2 NL/45s
        Right Side:
            3 NL/45s
            2 Barracuda Missiles
        Left Side:
            3 NL/45s
            2 Barracuda Missiles
    Middle Section
        Right Side:
            10 Medium Naval PPCs
        Left Side:
            10 Medium Naval PPCs

Engine Section
    Right Side:
        10 Medium Naval PPCs
        4 NL/45s
    Left Side:
        10 Medium Naval PPCs
        4 NL/45s
    Engine:
        4 Barracuda Missiles

Mass: 1,560,000 tons
Crew: 702
K-F Drive System: KF Tiger I
Interplanetary Engines: 3 Rolls Royce Krakens
Hull: Galadin SYN
  Length: 1,209 meters
  Sail Span: 1,375 meters
  DropShip Capacity: 6
  AeroSpace Fighter Capacity: 40
  Small Craft Complement: 16
Armor: Panthex YM1
Armament:
  16 Sunspot-3L Naval Particle Projection Cannon
  4 Killer Whale Missile Tubes
  2 Winchester-Boeing Autocannon
  48 Omicron-45 Series Heavy Naval Lasers
  6 Maelstrom AR-12 Missile Tubes
Manufacturer: Krester's Ship Construction
Communications System: Pathfinder 43CD
Targeting and Tracking System: MORSAT

Overview:

As venerated as the *Monsoon* battleship had become by the beginning of the 27th century, it was clear that countless upgrades and refits would not keep the class operational forever. Ships built for the private navies of the Member States, such as the Free World League's *Atreus* Class battleship, rivaled the *Monsoon*'s firepower and were easier to build and maintain.

In 2611, the admirals of the Star League Navy began listing characteristics they considered vital for a battleship. First and foremost was the need for more speed. During the *Monsoon*'s career, engine technology had made great steps forward in thrust capabilities, size, and serviceability.

Increased protection was another important requirement for the new battleship. Weapon technology had also advanced since the *Monsoon*'s creation, leaving what had been considered ample armor now suspect.

Lastly, the Star League Navy wanted a new ship to carry the largest and most advanced weapon systems available.

After much competition between shipbuilders, the admirals of Warship Sub-Command deliberated and awarded the contract to Krester's Ship Construction in late 2616. The design they came up with was for the *Texas.*

Capabilities:

The ship's hull took advantage of the new technologies. The lighter and stronger armor plating, a product of synthetic metals and BattleMech armor research, rides a frame that was less likely to succumb to stresses, yet still allowed more room for the ship's systems and crew.

The Communal XXX designed by the Nirasaki Computers Collective is one of the largest computers ever built, as powerful as planet-based machines that control communication and power grids.

The *Texas* carries a powerful array of weapons, the most spectacular being the two Winchester-Boeing Autocannon. With a muzzle diameter of almost two meters, these autocannon can throw 1.2-ton shells hundreds of kilometers with great accuracy. The size of these projectiles limits the number the *Texas* can carry, one of the ship's few faults. The ship has six missile launchers that can fire any size missiles, and it can carry 40 fighters. Along with PPCs and lasers, this assortment gives the *Texas* battleships a fearsome offensive capability. This weaponry and strength, combined with the maneuverability provided by its three Rolls Kraken engines, make the *Texas* battleship one of the most potent vessels of its time.

Construction of a *Texas* battleship, although aided extensively by automation, takes 18 months, almost twice the time needed to build the *Monsoon* battleships. As a result, Krester's Ship Construction has turned out only 52 of these vessels.

Type: **Texas**
Class: Battleship
Structural Integrity: 85
K-F Drive Integrity: 30
Energy Collector Sail Integrity: 5
Docking Hard Points: 6
Small Craft Cubicles: 56
Small Craft Bay Doors: 12
Grav Deck: 3
Engine: Rolls Royce Kraken
    Thrust: 3
    Overthrust: 5
    Fuel (1 Thrust Point/2 tons): 700
    Consumption: 39.52 tons/burn-day
Armor Factor (10 points/ton): 17,850
    Command Section
        Nose: 1,425
        Right Side: 2,500
        Left Side: 2,500
    Middle Section
        Right Side: 2,500
        Left Side: 2,500
    Engine Section
        Right Side: 2,500
        Left Side: 2,500
        Aft (engine): 1,425

Weapons:
    Command Section (Nose Firing Arc)
        Nose: None
        Right Side:
            4 Heavy Naval PPCs
            2 Killer Whale Missiles
            1 NAC/40
        Left Side:
            4 Heavy Naval PPCs
            2 Killer Whale Missiles
            1 NAC/40
    Middle Section
        Right Side:
            12 NL/45s
            2 AR-12s
        Left Side:
            12 NL/45s
            2 AR-12s

Engine Section
    Right Side:
        12 NL/45s
        1 AR-12
        4 Heavy Naval PPCs
    Left Side:
        12 NL/45s
        1 AR-12
        4 Heavy Naval PPCs
    Engine:
        None

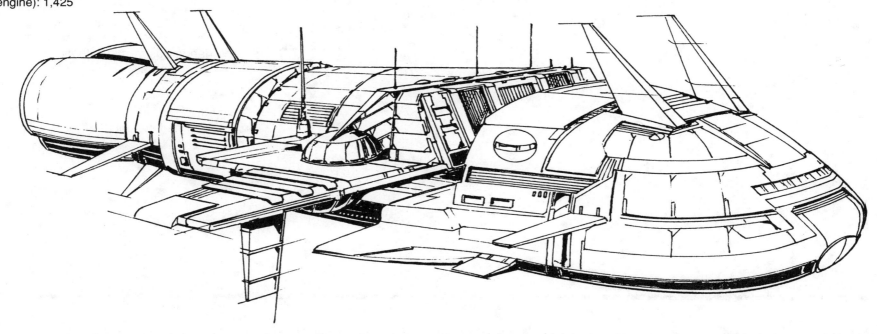

MCKENNA

Mass: 1,930,000 tons
Crew: 578
K-F Drive System: FK King I
Interplanetary Engines: 3 Goliath LV9s
Hull: Cortex UltraBond
   Length: 1,405 meters
   Sail Span: 1,560 meters
   DropShip Capacity: 6
   AeroSpace Fighter Capacity: 50
   Small Craft Complement: 16
Armor: Ulston C5-A
Armament:
   12 Zeus-40 Series Naval Autocannon
   12 Thunderbolt-55 Series Naval Lasers
   6 Maelstrom AR-10 Missile Systems
   48 Kreuss XX Particle Projection Cannon
Manufacturer: Blue Nose Clipperships
Communications System: Mercury TY60
Targeting and Tracking System: Communal V-1a

Overview:

The silhouette of angular turrets, mazes of towering sensor islands, and the sheer size of the *McKenna* battleship (twice as long as the previous largest JumpShip and ten times its mass) have made it one of the most recognizable warships. Sailors consider it the highlight of their careers to serve on one of the 280 ships of this class, and admirals invariably choose it as their flagship.

The *McKenna* was the only ship to win two consecutive Martial Olympiads, in 2696 and 2700.

Capabilities:

Proven reliability and major innovations won this prestigious and lucrative contract for the Blue Nose Clipperships of Mars. Reliability came from the fact that the ship's hull was based on the *Farragut* battleship, the strongest and most stress-resistant previous design.

The *McKenna* Class battleship carries the Lithium-Fusion battery system, a proven system after more than a century of use, even though few warships carry it because of its great expense. The L-F system stores energy in its series of Tokomak Rings, collecting it from the ship's sail or from a space station. The ship can jump into a star system, find itself surrounded, and use the energy in the L-F batteries to make the immediate jump back to a friendly star system.

The *McKenna* carries an unprecedented number and variety of weapons. Many naval officers feared at first that the large number and type of weapons would be unreliable in battle or would tax the ship's fire-control computers. The Communal V Naval Combat Computer System, from the Nirasaki Computers Collective, proved to be powerful enough for the ship's weapons, most of which worked well. The only exception was the balky Maelstrom missile system, which can launch any type of missile. Successive versions failed to meet expectations until the Maelstrom AR-10 finally worked properly.

The *McKenna* can carry many more AeroSpace Fighters than its predecessors, and it also holds six DropShips, marking a major shift in naval doctrine. Before the *McKenna*, the SLDF considered battleships huge escorts for combat transports. The *McKenna* can carry two regiments of ground forces and AeroSpace Fighters and can train most of its weapons on a planet's surface, giving the Star League the ability to use a single ship to quell all but the most dangerous military situation on a planet.

Type: **McKenna**
Class: Battleship
Structural Integrity: 95
K-F Drive Integrity: 35
Energy Collector Sail Integrity: 6
Docking Hard Points: 6
Small Craft Cubicles: 66
Small Craft Bay Doors: 12
Grav Deck: 3
Engine: Goliath LV-9
   Thrust: 3
   Overthrust: 5
   Fuel (1 Thrust Point/2 tons): 800
   Consumption: 39.52 tons/burn-day
Armor Factor (8points/ton): 12,839
   Command Section
      Nose: 1,300
      Right Side: 1,800
      Left Side: 1,800
   Middle Section
      Right Side: 1,800
      Left Side: 1,800
   Engine Section
      Right Side: 1,800
      Left Side: 1,800
      Aft (Engine): 739

Weapons:
   Command Section (Nose Firing Arc)
      Nose:
         2 NAC/40s
         2 NL/55s
      Right Side:
         3 NAC/40s
         3 NL/55s
         2 AR-10s
      Left Side:
         3 NAC/40s
         3 NL/55s
         2 AR-10s

Middle Section
   Right Side:
      12 Naval PPCs
   Left Side:
      12 Naval PPCs
Engine Section
   Right Side:
      12 Naval PPCs
   Left Side :
      12 Naval PPCs
   Engine:
      4 NAC/40s
      4 NL/55s
      2 AR-10s

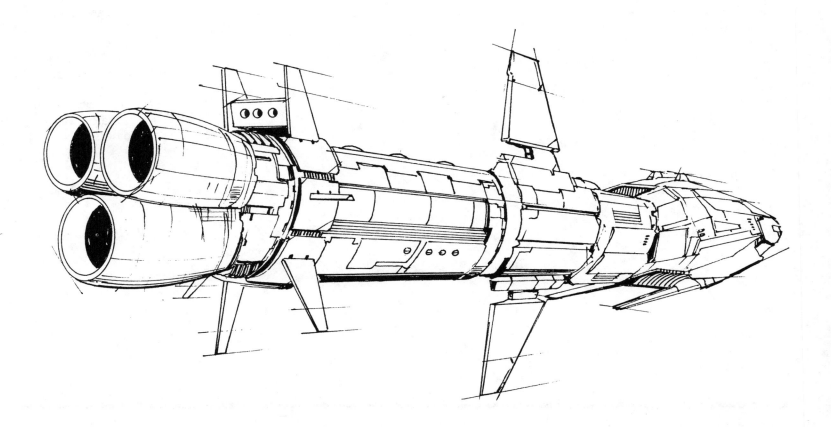

CONFEDERATE

Mass: 1860 tons
Crew: 10
Engine: 1 Thordan 650X
Hull: EndoSteel AN
    Height: 32.6 meters
    Width: 36.4 meters
    AeroSpace Fighter Capacity: 2/0
    BattleMech Complement: 4/6
Armament:
    14 Thunderbolt DT Large Lasers
    20 Harmon Medium Lasers
Armor: Ferro-Tile 87
Manufacturer: Kong Interstellar
Communications System: Rander 200
Targeting and Tracking System: Rander TA-5

Overview:

The *Confederate* Class DropShip is the Star League Defense Forces' standard BattleMech lance transport. Though not known for its aesthetic appeal, it is highly efficient at delivering 'Mechs to combat situations.

Being an energy-based transport, a *Confederate* can remain in the field for extended periods of time, and is often called on to provide supporting fire for AeroSpace Fighter wings. It carries an array of lasers for offensive operations when unloading 'Mechs in the heat of battle.

Capabilities:

The *Confederate* boasts one of the most advanced engine bays in the SLDF. The reliable, efficient drive system takes up less than 20 percent of the ship's available room and weighs almost 10 percent less than its predecessor. Maintenance requirements are high, but the extra room aboard ship makes it less time-consuming than on other warships. Maintenance on 'Mechs is also made more efficient by the extensive repair equipment, cargo lifters, replacement armor, myomer bundles, and electronic components.

The fighter bays are twice the size of the 'Mech bays and many times more versatile. They can carry either AeroSpace Fighters, BattleMechs, or cargo, with areas prearranged for takeoff and landing Fighters, cocoons for landing 'Mechs, and extra room for cargo.

The bridge and crew quarters are spartan but functional, as the space lavished on hardware is taken in part from personnel areas. Though quarters are cramped, most soldiers agree that transport aboard a *Confederate* is less difficult than on some others.

Type: **Confederate**
Class: DropShip
Structural Integrity: 8
Fighter Decks: 2
Fighter Bay Doors: 2
'Mech Cubicles: 4
'Mech Bay Doors: 4
Engine:
    Thrust: 4
    Overthrust: 6
    Fuel (12 Thrust Points/Ton): 135
    Consumption: 1.65 Tons/Burn Day
Armor Factor (16 points/ton): 46
    Nose   160
    Right Side   128
    Left Side   128
    Left Rear   128
    Right Rear 128
    Engine   64

Weapons
    Nose:
        2 Large Lasers
        2 Medium Lasers
    Each Side:
        3 Large Lasers
        5 Medium Lasers
    Each Rear Side:
        2 Large Lasers
        3 Medium Lasers
    Aft:
        2 Large Lasers
        2 Medium Lasers

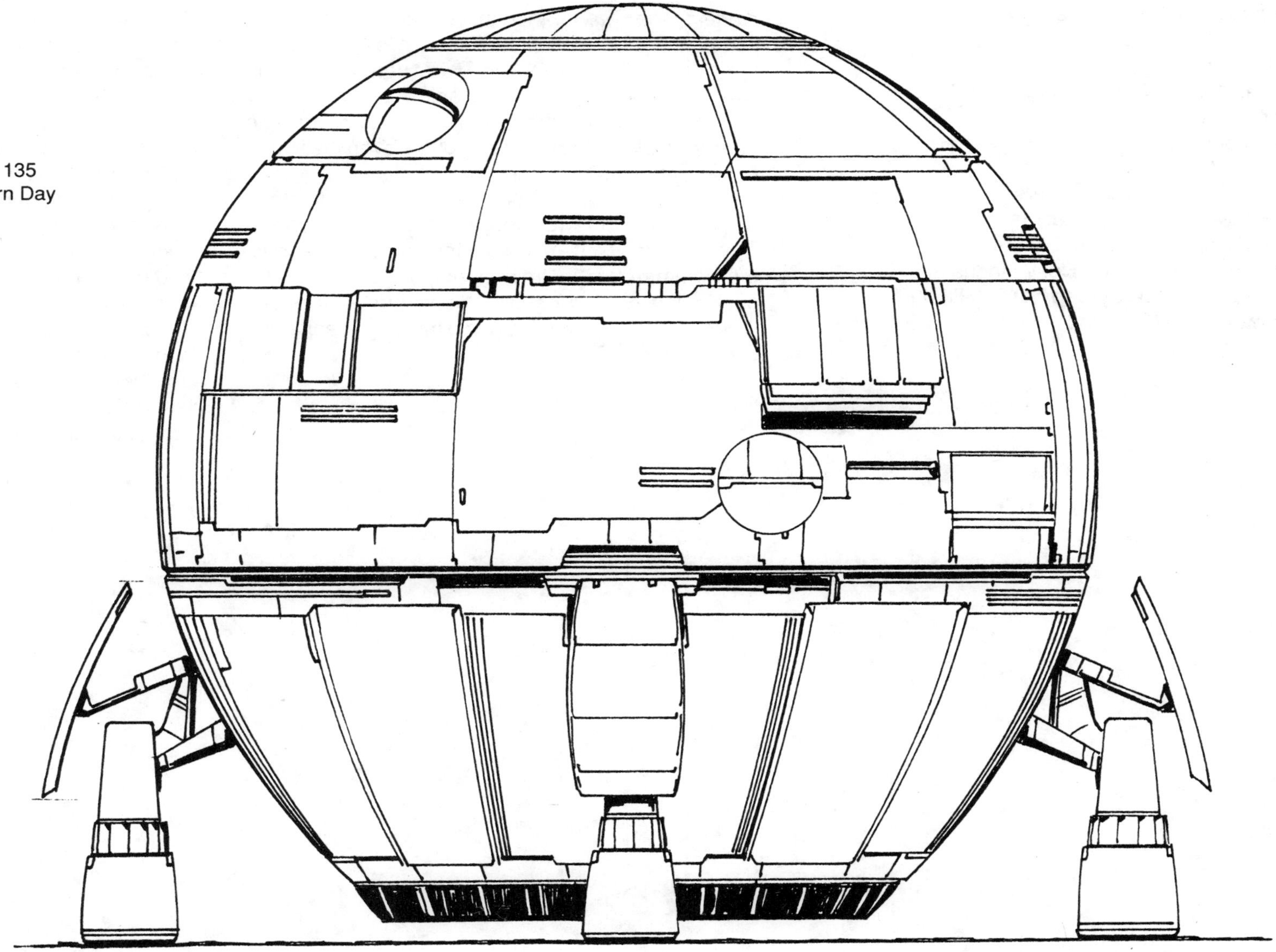

Mass: 12,000 tons
Crew: 10 Crew members, 18 AeroSpace Pilots
Engines: 3 GM 750-A12s
Hull:
   Length: 250 meters
   AeroSpace Fighter Capacity: 18
Armor: Starshield
Armament:
   8 Pontiac-20 Autocannon
   6 Delta-X LRM Launchers
   22 BlazeFire Large Lasers
   10 Hellion-b Medium Lasers
Manufacturer: Di Tron Heavy Industries
Communications System: O/P AIR500
Targeting and Tracking System: IMB SYS 3740

Overview:

One of the largest of the Star League's fighter carriers, the *Titan* can transport the entire fighter complement for a battalion. Though this places all the unit's eggs in one basket, the *Titan*'s heavy armor and strong engines make it a reliable enough delivery system to minimize the risk. The arrival of a single *Titan*'s shipload can, in fact, often overwhelm the fighter defenses of a jump point or planet.

The *Titan*'s only purpose is to deliver its fighters. Consequently, crews tend to be single-minded in performance of duty. The senior member of the crew, the Commander Air Group (CAG), is responsible for positioning the ship for take-off and retrieval in battle, though he has no say in running the ship in any other circumstance.

Capabilities:

The *Titan* was designed with AeroSpace Fighter pilots in mind, and they respond by seeking duty aboard this ship more than any other. Duty aboard this class is more dangerous than on other ships because the *Titan* tends to see so much action, but this is offset by the higher degree of creature comforts available to personnel.

The ship has a large bridge, which in addition to its normal ship functions, serves as tactical nerve center for the fighters in combat. Because the CAG takes the bridge to feed tactical information to each pilot, most air groups consider him or her to be the honorary nineteenth member of the Flight.

The ship contains three separate flight decks, each capable of housing six fighters. The integrity of each deck assures maximum damage-control efficiency. Each deck is equipped with one door each for take-off and landing.

Type: **Titan**
Class: Fighter Carrier
Structural Integrity: 7
AeroSpace Fighter Decks: 3
Bay Doors: 6
Engine:
    Thrust   5
    Overthrust   8
    Fuel (6 Thrust Points/Ton)   480
    Consumption   1.84 Tons/Burn-Day
Armor Factor (16 points/ton)   46
    Nose   192
    Right Wing   192
    Left Wing   192
    Fuselage   224
    Engine   208

Weapons	Location
AC/20	Nose
LRM-20	Nose
Large Laser	Nose
Large Laser	Nose
AC/20	Left Wing
AC/20	Left Wing
AC/20	Right Wing
AC/20	Right Wing
LRM/20	Right Wing
LRM/20	Left Wing
Large Laser	Left Wing
Large Laser	Left Wing
Large Laser	Left Wing
Large Laser	Left Wing
Large Laser	Right Wing
Large Laser	Right Wing
Large Laser	Right Wing
Large Laser	Right Wing
Medium Laser	Left Wing
Medium Laser	Left Wing
Medium Laser	Left Wing
Medium Laser	Left Wing
Medium Laser	Right Wing
Medium Laser	Right Wing
Medium Laser	Right Wing
Medium Laser	Right Wing
AC/20	Fuselage
AC/20	Fuselage
LRM-20	Fuselage
LRM-20	Fuselage
Large Laser	Fuselage
Large Laser	Fuselage
Large Laser	Fuselage
Large Laser	Fuselage
Large Laser	Fuselage
Large Laser	Fuselage
Large Laser	Fuselage
Large Laser	Fuselage
Large Laser	Fuselage
AC/20	Aft
LRM-20	Aft
Medium Laser	Aft
Medium Laser	Aft
Medium Laser	Aft
Medium Laser	Aft

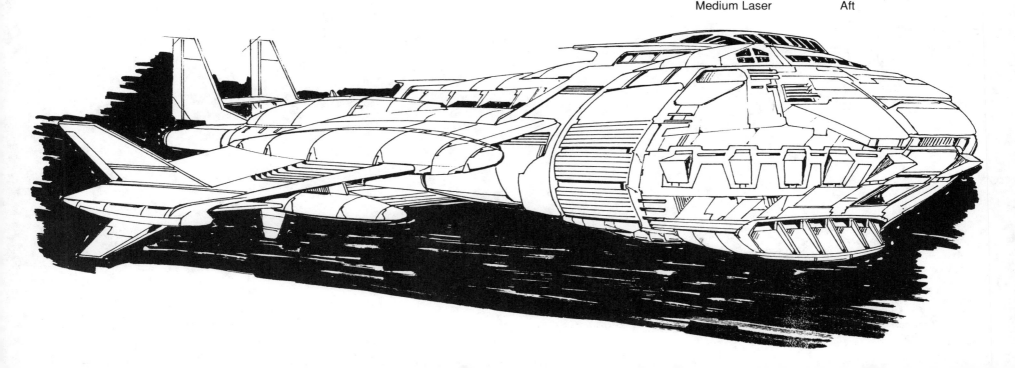

PERSONAL EQUIPMENT

Emergency Jetpack

Many situations call for a lightweight emergency jetpack that will allow a person to escape combat or some other dangerous event. BanderGaff Technologies Limited introduced the No. 5 Jump Pack as a solution. More than 10,000 of these disposable systems are used throughout the Star League Defense Forces and various private concerns.

The system is a relatively simply one. The pack is small, about the size of a suitcase, and very light. It contains a solid rocket propellant and a hand-held electronic control system. The pack can lift 280 kilograms for 1 kilometer at a height of 30 meters. Maximum horizontal speed is approximately 160 kph.

It takes less than a minute to put on the pack and activate it. The control system is hard-wired to the pack, and the No. 5 Pack is disposable after use. Once activated, it takes only 5 seconds to ignite. Once fired, the system cannot be shut off.

Many foot soldiers have such packs stored nearby in case they are overrun and driven into an emergency retreat. Many agents of the Star League have been known to carry such packs concealed within luggage in case of desperate situations. The system has proven very dependable.

Type: Bander Gaff Technologies No. 5 Emergency Jump Pack
Cost: 5,000 Star League Dollars
Weight: 5 kilograms

Game Use

The Emergency Jetpack uses all of the jetpack rules found on Page 62 of **MechWarrior**, with the following exceptions. Maximum altitude is 30 meters, and maximum distance flown is 1 kilometer. The Emergency Jetpack can be used only once.

EMP Pulse Mines

The EMP Pulse Mine acts just as a Vibrabomb. It is buried just below the surface and is set for a particular weight of BattleMech. Its area of effect is equal to only one hex in **BattleTech** due to the unique nature of this device. The EMP Pulse Mine is actually a low yield micro-fusion bomb. When set off, it generates a controlled, high energy Electro-Magnetic Pulse. The actual explosion is minor, but the EMP blast can cripple any BattleMech in the same hex.

Type: EMP Pulse Mine
Cost: 5,000 Star League Dollars
Weight: 50 kilograms

Game Use

The EMP Pulse Mine uses all of the Vibrabomb rules found on Page 45 of the **BattleTech Manual**. When the mine detonates, roll 2D6 for each 'Mech in the same hex. On a 7 or higher, the unit is shut down for 1D6 turns of play until the battle computer and sensors are brought back on line. The MechWarrior must roll against his *Piloting* Skill if the 'Mech was moving to see if it falls over. The explosion of the mine causes no damage, but damage from falling applies as normal.

The main drawback to the EMP Pulse Mine is its high cost. This has restricted its use except around permanent Star League facilities and storage centers.

BANDERGAFF TECH. #5 JUMP PACK BACK PACK COVER REMOVED FOR CLARITY

PULSE MINE

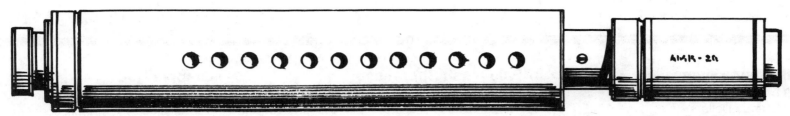

AMR-20 RIFLE / PISTOL SILENCER

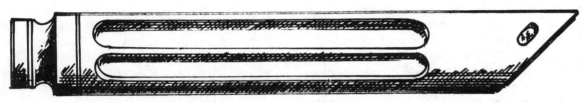

JAF-05 FLASH SURPRESSOR

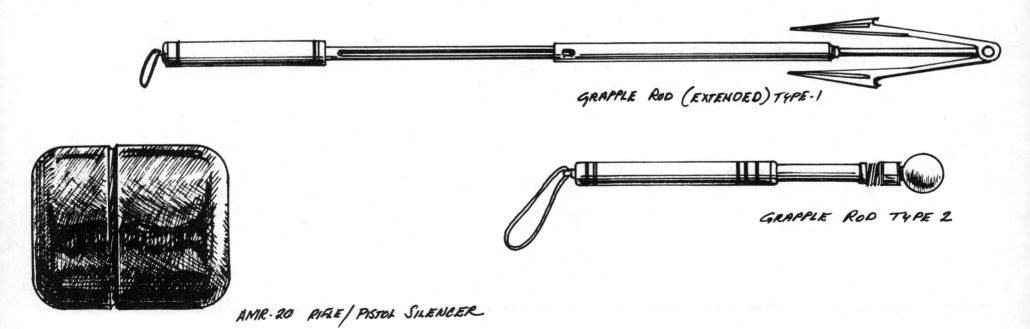

GRAPPLE ROD (EXTENDED) TYPE-1

GRAPPLE ROD TYPE 2

AMR-20 RIFLE / PISTOL SILENCER

AMR-20 Rifle/Pistol Silencer

Type: AMR-20 Rifle/Pistol Silencer
Cost: 500 Star League Dollars
Weight: 50 grams

Game Use

To determine if a character has heard a weapon equipped with an AMR-20, make a LRN Saving Roll, using the following table for modifiers.

Silencer Table			
	Short	Medium	Long
Modifier	0	+2	+4
Range	1-5	6-10	11+

JAF-05 Flash Suppressor

Jameson, Airmore, and Fiat, Inc. designed the Star League's sophisticated Flash Suppressor, the JAF-05. This system eliminates flash caused by the use of shell-firing rifles or grenade launchers. Furthermore, the JAF-05 can actually divert the "flash" caused by lasers. The absence of flash makes it more difficult for most BattleMech sensors to pick up the attacker's location.

The suppressor uses a prismatic deflector that catches the initial burst of photons produced when laser-beam energy ionizes air. It then diverts that light energy in the direction set in the suppressor. The high-flash photons are set to collide 30 meters from where the laser was fired. The direction that the light can be channeled is adjusted by turning the entire suppressor assembly, and so it can be diverted down, up or at some angle. The system is simple and has few moving parts, requiring little maintenance.

Type: JAF-05 Flash Suppressor
Cost: 1,000 Star League Dollars
Weight: 50 grams

Game Use

If a weapon is fired in the dark, a character will immediately see the muzzle flash. However, characters must make a LRN Saving Roll to spot the muzzle flash of a weapon equipped with a JAF-05 Flash Suppressor. The following table should be used for modifiers.

Spotting Table			
	Close	Medium	Long
Modifier	0	+2	+4
Range	1-10	11-20	21+

Grapple Rod

The Grapple Rod is a disposable tool for climbing a surface quickly. Its most common use is by infantry fighting against 'Mechs. A Grapple Rod is a shaft one meter long with a ball at one end and a small strap at the other. Controls are at the middle of the shaft. The ball is made of adhesive material, attached to 10 meters of lightweight nylon/myomer cable.

A soldier places his foot in the strap and depresses the lift button. A charge within the shaft fires the adhesive ball at the target. Once the ball is attached, the soldier activates another button, which causes a motor in the device to activate, pulling the shaft and the rider up the cable to the location of the adhesive. The infantryman can perform his mission and ride the cable back to the ground.

This tactic is used by infantry to swarm a BattleMech. Two squads can board a passing 'Mech in seconds, planting explosives and firing at vital areas. They quickly slide off the 'Mech and detonate the explosives.

Type: Grapple Rod
Cost: 500 Star League Dollars
Skill Class: Rifle
Weight: 1.7 kilograms
Range in Hexes: 2

To use the Grapple Rod, the player should make a personal weapons attack during the Ranged Weapon Attack Phase of the turn. The attack is at close range, and all other combat modifiers apply. If the Grapple Rod hits its target, the player may spend 1 MP during the next movement phase and ride the device to the target. It costs 2 MP to ride back down. Going up and down can be done during the same movement phase as long as the character has sufficient MP.

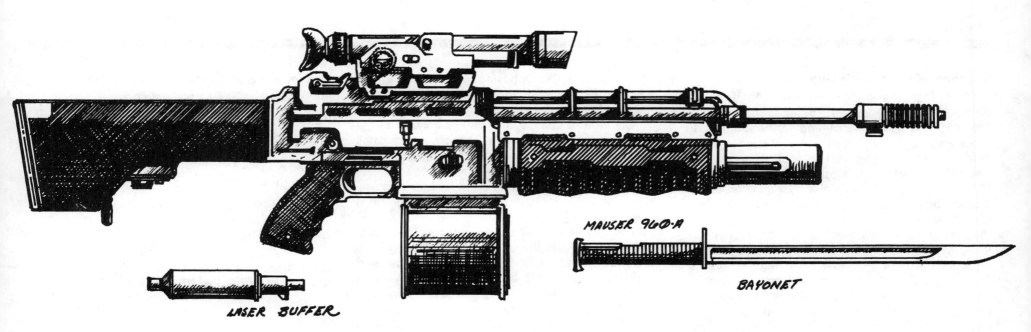

MAUSER 960·A

LASER BUFFER

BAYONET

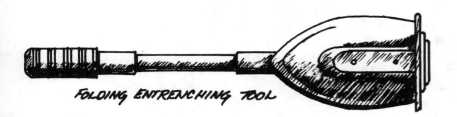

FOLDING ENTRENCHING TOOL

FLARE, TYPE

FLARE, TYPE J

LONG·BURNING FLARES

NYLON CABLE
(5 METERS)

FLASHLIGHT

PULSE SIGNAL STICK

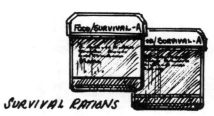

FOOD/SURVIVAL-A

SURVIVAL RATIONS

Mauser 960 Assault System

The infantry trooper of the Star League is the best-outfitted and -trained soldier in history. The Mauser 960 is the standard firearm of the infantryman in the Regular Army. It is a weapon designed for an extended campaign against a variety of opponents; BattleMechs, vehicles, fighters, or other infantry. More importantly, it is a reliable system of firepower that is compact and easy to care for in the worst circumstances.

The primary feature of the weapon is the pulse laser system. It is supplemented by an auto-grenade launcher that fires grenades weighing 210 grams. The Mauser 960 also contains a survival pack within its stock. It has a vibro-blade mounted as a bayonet and a sight for accurate fire. In general, it provides a wide variety of weapons that the infantryman can utilize in combat against an assortment of opposing forces.

The grenade launcher can be fired as a single shot or in automatic mode. The grenade mix can consist of the usual explosive, flash (affecting the hex hit), smoke (affecting the hex hits), thermite (causing fire on the struck object/opponent) or can be used to fire Thumper Rounds, which are unique to the Mauser 960. They explode with an adhesive that attaches a solar powered transmitter that signals the enemy's position. This marks opposing BattleMechs for attacks by fighters and other more heavily armed forces.

The Vibro-Blade Bayonet can be activated from the trigger system on the rifle. There is a very small explosive charge in the mount that allows the infantryman to fire the bayonet at an attacking enemy. The range of this is limited, only eight meters with any degree of accuracy, but it is another element in a universal fighting system.

The survival kit, with the exception of the folding spade, is stored in the stock of the weapon. The emergency flares are long-burning and can be used as torches or as ways to start fires. The battery life on the flashlight is 48 hours of use. The rations consist of pill packages, and the medical kit is only a one-meter bandage and a small aerosol disinfectant. The hollow stock can carry extra power clips or other weapons as well. The firing mechanisms for the auto-grenade launcher and the pulse laser are the same and can be activated at the touch of a single button.

The only disadvantage to the weapon is its weight. It does not weigh as much as many of the large GyroJet rifles, but it is still a bulky device to carry for a long time. Its mix of firepower allows the Mauser 960 to operate in a variety of roles in combat, making it a favorite of generals and the common soldier alike.

Mauser 960 Star League Assault System
Weight: 9.8 Kilograms (Unloaded)

Pulse Laser
Power Usage: 2
Skill Class: Rifle
Damage: 3D6+3
Range in Hexes:

Short	1 – 7
Medium	8 – 15
Long	16 – 30

Reload Time: 1 turn

Auto-Grenade Launcher
Number of Shots Per Clip: 6
Skill Class: Rifle
Damage: 2D6+3
Range in Hexes:

Short	1 – 6
Medium	7 – 15
Long	16 – 25

Area of Effect: 1 Hex
Reload Time: 2 turns

Survival Equipment:
Folding Spade
2 Long-Burning Emergency Flares
Pulse Signal Stick
2 Packages of Emergency Nutrition Supplements
5 Meters of Nylon Cable
Flashlight
Wrap Bandage and Spray

Extra Equipment:
Modified Vibro-Blade Bayonet
UV/Starlight Scope

MechWarrior's Combat Suit

The MechWarrior's Combat Suit was developed for the personal guards of House Kurita. The suit is a multifunctional, full-body unit, complete with a specially designed neurohelmet for BattleMech control. The MCS provides the wearer with a powerful integral cooling system to combat the high temperatures inside a 'Mech's cockpit. This cooling system is designed into a close-fitting, flexible undersuit. The outside of the suit is covered by a strong, heat-resistant polymer fabric that protects the wearer from shrapnel and some small arms fire. Additionally, a rigid vest fits over the chest to further protect the pilot.

The helmet not only provides the neurolink between pilot and 'Mech, but it also encloses the pilots head, providing a constant supply of fresh air from the cockpit's life support system through a set of connecting lines in the side of the helmet. These lines also link the helmet's communications gear into the 'Mech's powerful main systems. When these lines disconnect, the helmet's internal systems automatically take over, providing breathable air through a 6-hour internal supply, and 12 hours of communications time using the small integral communicator, which has a 10-kilometer range.

Another standard feature of the suit is its provision for the attachment of the MechWarrior's Combat Medipack. This unit attaches to a hook-up point on the wearer's thigh and monitors the pilot's condition, automatically injecting any necessary combination of pain killer and stimulants to keep the pilot functioning.

Game Use

The MechWarrior's Combat Suit absorbs one-fourth of all damage taken by the wearer from slug-throwing and melee weapons and 4 points of damage from energy weapons. The suit loses its effectiveness after absorbing a total of 16 points. If the rigid vest is worn over the suit, it stops one-half of all damage taken to the wearer's chest from slug-throwing weapons and 4 points of damage from energy weapons, in addition to damage absorbed by the suit itself. The suit reduces the wearer's movement by one-fourth, but the rigid vest imposes no further penalties. The neurohelmet stops 15 points of damage to the wearer's head.

MediPack

The MediPack is a thin box, contoured to attach to a MechWarrior's thigh, either strapped to the leg or hooked to a suit. The device was designed for use by the personal guard of Takiro Kurita, though Medi-Packs have become common among many other House and Regular Army units.

The device monitors the wearer's vital statistics with several sensors attached to the wearer's skin. The unit determines if the wearer needs pain killers or stimulants and administers them as necessary.

The unit weighs only 400 grams and has a built-in power supply that keeps it operating for up to 48 hours without recharging. The unit recharges by plugging into a power line in the BattleMech's cockpit, but medications must be replaced at least once a month even if the pilot used none of the twelve doses.

Type: MediPack
Cost: 400 Star League Dollars
Weight: .4 kilograms

Game Use

When the MediPack is set to keep the wearer conscious, it uses one dose of stimulant each time the wearer fails any Consciousness Saving Roll. Each time this occurs, the player takes 1D6 of additional damage. This damage goes directly against the character's HTK, affecting any future Consciousness Rolls. The unit will not inject a dose if the character has 6 or fewer points remaining. However, the player may override it and force the injection if he so desires.

FIELD DRESSING KIT

Model 15 Gripper Gloves

Gripper Gloves came from the laboratories of BabTech on the planet Clinton in the Lyran Commonwealth. These gloves are uncommonly thick, nearly 1 cm overall. They have large gauntlets that come almost half-way up the forearms of those wearing them. Each glove has its own power supply that provides several hours of continuous use.

Each glove can generate a hyper-sonic field in the fingertips. This field has a very low frequency and gauges itself automatically for the surface that it is being applied against. When pressed against virtually any surface, the gloves adhere to the surface, supporting 150 kilograms each. A control built into the thumb of the glove deactivates the field.

Model 15 gloves are manufactured with myomer bundling and give the user an incredible amount of strength in the fingers and hands. The wearer can crush small rocks, force doors open, and so on. The gloves weigh almost 1 kilogram themselves and are somewhat bulky, but many consider this a small price to pay for their capabilities. The Model 15 gloves, though expensive, have become a favorite among thieves, who use them to scale sheer surfaces.

The Special Forces of the Star League Defense Forces are the principal purchasers of the Model 15 Gripper Gloves. Used in assaults and especially in city warfare, the gloves have proven invaluable. Their only weakness is the amount of training required to use weapons or tools without crushing them. True experts can catch a bottle tossed to them without cracking or breaking it.

Type: Model 15 Gripper Gloves
Cost: 1,000 Star League Dollars
Weight: 1 kilogram

Game Use

Characters wearing the Gripper Gloves have their DEX reduced by 1. However, the amount of Brawling damage that a character does increases by 2. Characters may also use the Gripper Gloves to scale a vertical surface. Move as if crawling, expending 1 MP for every floor (5 meters) traveled up or down.

Vibro Lock Pick Kit

The Vibro Lock Pick Kit is a small vibro blade with a limited power supply that is used for operations that require cutting locks. Small, slender, and easily concealed, the Vibro Lock Pick Kit is standard equipment for intelligence agents on clandestine operations. Vibroblade technology is not new, but the compact design and power of this system are rare.

Powered by a small photoelectric cell and battery, the blade can operate for less than a minute, and it can take up to two hours of direct light to recharge. The blade extends out only 7.5cm, making it of little use in combat but the fear of every locksmith within the Star League.

Type: Vibro Lock Pick Kit
Cost: 2,000 Star League Dollars
Power Usage: 1/shot
Time to Recharge: 1 Turn
Weight: 100 grams

Game Use

The battery has 5 points of power available to it. It takes 2 hours in direct sunlight to fully recharge the Lock Pick. Using the Vibro Lock Pick adds a −5 modifier to any lock picking attempt. The Vibro Lock Pick cannot be used as a melee weapon.

GRIPPER GLOVE

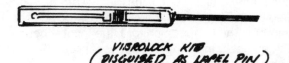

VIBROLOCK KIT
(DISGUISED AS LAPEL PIN)